DEMOCRACY
in the Middle East

DEFINING THE CHALLENGE

Contributors:

Joshua Muravchik
Laurie Mylroie
Graham Fuller
Martin Kramer
Mohammed Abdelbeki Hermassi

Edited by Yehudah Mirsky and Matt Ahrens

A WASHINGTON INSTITUTE MONOGRAPH

Library of Congress Cataloging-in-Publication Data

Democracy in the Middle East: defining the
challenge/ edited by Yehudah Mirsky and Matt
Ahrens ; contributors, Josh Muravchik ... [et al.].
        p.   cm.
     "A Washington Institute Monograph."
     ISBN 0-944029-53-1
        1. Democracy—Middle East. 2. Middle East—
Politics and government—1979- 3. United States—
Foreign Relations—Middle East. 4. Middle East—
Foreign Relations—United States. I. Mirsky,
Yehudah. II. Ahrens, Matt. III. Muravchik, Joshua.
IV. Washington Institute for Near East Policy.
JQ1758.A91D46   1993
321.8′0956--dc20   93-28820
                                                CIP

Copyright © 1993 by
The Washington Institute for Near East Policy
1828 L Street, N.W., Suite 1050
Washington, D.C. 20036
Library of Congress Catalog Card Number: 93-28820
ISBN 0-944029-53-1

Cover Design by Jill Indyk
Cover photograph © Gregoire/EEA/SABA
October 1992 Borj–Mlain, Algeria
A FIS RALLY

CONTENTS

CONTRIBUTORS

Graham Fuller, a senior political scientist at the RAND Corporation, served as the National Intelligence Officer for the Near East and South Asia responsible for long-range intelligence forecasting from 1982 to 1986. Previously, he held a number of diplomatic and intelligence posts in the Middle East. A frequent commentator on Middle Eastern and Central Asian politics, he is author of *The Democracy Trap: Perils of the Post-Cold War World* (1992).

Mohammed Abdelbeki Hermassi, a sociologist and former chairman of the Tunisian Political and Social Studies Association, has served since September 1992 as Tunisia's permanent representative to United Nations Educational, Scientific, and Cultural Organization. Dr. Hermassi was previously the vice dean of the University of Tunis, and taught for eight years at the University of California at Berkeley. His writings on Islamic politics and the challenges of political reform in North Africa include *L'Islam Protestaire* (1986), *Societe et Islam dans le Maghreb Arabe* (1987), and *Le Maghreb Face aux Mutations Internationales* (forthcoming).

Martin Kramer is the associate director of the Moshe Dayan Center for Middle Eastern and African Studies at Tel Aviv University, a member of the advisory board of the *Oxford Encyclopedia of the Modern Islamic World*, and a former visiting fellow at The Washington Institute. Among his many published works on aspects of political Islam are *Islam*

Assembled (1986), *Shi'ism, Resistance and Revolution* (1987), *Hezbollah's Vision of the West* (Washington Institute Policy Paper No. 16), and *Islam, Democracy, and the Peace Process* (forthcoming, Washington Institute Policy Paper).

Joshua Muravchik is a resident scholar at the American Enterprise Institute for Public Policy Research and an adjunct scholar of The Washington Institute. One of the foremost thinkers on the roles of democracy and human rights in U.S. foreign policy, he is the author of *The Uncertain Crusade: Jimmy Carter and the Dilemmas of Human Rights Policy* (1986) and *Exporting Democracy: Fulfilling America's Destiny* (1991).

Laurie Mylroie is an Arab affairs fellow at The Washington Institute. She has previously taught in the Department of Government at Harvard University and at the U.S. Naval War College. A leading expert on Iraqi politics and regional security in the Persian Gulf, she is the author of *Saddam Hussein and the Crisis in the Gulf* (with Judith Miller, 1990), *The Future of Iraq* (Washington Institute Policy Paper No. 24), and *Iraq: Options for U.S. Policy* (Washington Institute Policy Focus No. 21).

•   •   •

The contributions in this monograph are edited versions of presentations delivered to a Washington Institute policy forum on March 18, 1993. Dr. Hermassi delivered his presentation at a special policy forum on March 30, 1993.

PREFACE

The promotion of democracy abroad, long a major tenet of U.S. foreign policy, has taken on newfound importance in the wake of the Soviet Union's collapse. President Clinton has promised to make the promotion of democracy a key element of his foreign policy. The Middle East, a region where autocratic regimes are the rule, has been largely untouched by the wave of democratization in recent years. Indeed, it may be the one area of the world where a key element of democracy, i.e., popular elections, may generate as many problems as it solves, especially if it results in the displacement of undemocratic yet friendly regimes by anti-Western Islamist forces which, once in power, may eliminate future elections and other facets of democracy—in essence "one man, one vote, one time."

These ambiguities have led some analysts to conclude that the U.S. foreign policy ideal of promoting democracy abroad should not apply to the Middle East. Others argue that we should not give up on the democratic ideal but that it should be pursued cautiously or instituted only in stages.

To help further this discussion, The Washington Institute convened a panel of experts to discuss the feasibility, desirability and implications of promoting democratization in the Middle East and the problems and opportunities such a policy poses to U.S. interests in the region. These proceedings, together with the many documents gathered in the appendix to this volume, help define that challenge.

Mike Stein   Barbi Weinberg
President   Chairman

EXPORTING DEMOCRACY TO
THE ARAB WORLD

Joshua Muravchik

Democracy is immensely desirable in the Middle East, and in the Arab world in particular, for the sake of the Arabs, for the sake of the Israelis and, one could say, for the sakes of America and the rest of the world, as well.

For the sake of the Arabs, because it is axiomatic that democracy is desirable for people everywhere, even people who have had no history or experience with democracy. There is much recent empirical evidence that people do in fact want democracy and are willing to fight for it, even in obscure corners of the world where conventional skepticism or cynicism once said there would be little or no interest in it.

It also seems a logical axiom that one cannot force people to be free against their will. Sometimes it is said that people in some nondemocratic parts of the world do not want democracy; it is not their way; it is not their style, or tradition, or culture or what have you.

But it is logically self-contradictory to say that people do not want democracy. This is because unless one starts with the assumption that people ought to be able to get what they want, which is the basic assumption of democracy, what is the relevance of what they want? Once the question of what people want is invoked, you have already started with a premise that what people want is what they are entitled to have.

In a democratic setting, political participation is not compulsory; that is, if most people in a democratic setting really do not want democracy, they do not have to exercise their democratic rights. They are not forced to speak up, and they can allow others to decide and speak for them, if they so choose. There is, in other words, no possibility of doing anyone harm by offering them a democratic choice.

Rather, the more familiar and real danger is just the opposite; that people who want the authority to be their own masters and determine their own lives will be denied that by others through the use of coercion.

With respect to the Arab world, I think democracy is desirable because the Arab world seems so unhappy. That is, Arab politics seems to be driven by a relentless spirit of grievance and self-pity, and a sense of having been victims and that the Arab's fate has been determined by others.

One key to the Arab world's finding some of the maturity, health, and happiness that has eluded it is the process of people taking and accepting responsibility for their own situation, and their own destinies. And the only way people can do that is in a democratic system in which they can be their own masters.

Arab democracy is desirable as well for the sake of Israel. Israel needs to maintain its military strength to defend itself, and to reach peace with its Arab neighbors if that is possible. But for the long run, the survival of Israel depends on its eventually being accepted by its neighbors in the region where it is located. This would, for the first time, enable it to move toward a more normal life, rather than having to be a state perpetually armed to the teeth and on alert against would-be attackers.

The key to that deliverance could well be the democratization of the Arab world. There is a great deal of research, familiar to everyone, that shows that democracies get into war much less often than dictatorships, and particularly not with each other. This was theorized about even before there were any democracies, by Immanuel Kant, who offered the logical explanation that, if people who have to do the fighting and dying are the ones who make the decisions, there will be fewer wars.

But there is actually a deeper explanation for this. Democracy is, at bottom, not just a political system, but an ethic that maintains that it is more important to make decisions in the right way than to get one's own way. It embodies the idea that differences should be resolved, not through violence, but through talking, voting and other forms of civic life.

There is, then, a very real connection inherent in the notion that, in their relations with their fellow citizens, people should resolve arguments without killing each other, and the notion that, in relations with other states, they should resolve arguments without recourse to war.

This connection was put most eloquently and beautifully by Alexander Solzhenitsyn in his very first speech in America after he came out of the Soviet Union. Trying to rally the West to recognize the enormity of the Soviet menace, he went through a blood-chilling litany of the executions and barbarities perpetuated by the Soviet regime against its own citizens. And then, at the end of this litany, he turned to the audience and said, "What makes you think they will treat you any better?" That, it seems to me, is precisely the point.

There is, then, a long-term relationship between the prospect for peace in the Middle East and the prospect of democracy there. But, of course, that brings us to the next question, namely, is democracy possible in the Arab world? We know that there are now no Arab democracies. There are a small number of Islamic democracies, but no Arab democracies. This leads some to conclude that, for whatever reason, it is simply not possible for democracy to take hold in this part of the world.

But this seems quite an unfounded inference. We have in the last two decades, beginning in 1974, witnessed an enormous tide of democratization that first began in southern Europe and then spread to Latin America and East Asia, and, with the collapse of communism, to Eastern Europe, the former Soviet Union and now even to Africa.

According to this year's count by Freedom House, there are eighty-five countries in the world that have, at this moment, democratic governments or, in Freedom House's terms, are "free" countries, including many countries in which the advent of democracy was not widely-anticipated: Nepal, Mongolia, Kirghizstan, Benin and so on.

Some say that a number of these countries that have recently joined democratic ranks have very shallow democratic roots and will probably revert to dictatorship sometime soon. No doubt some of them will. But a great many of the countries that we think of today as being stable democracies also had shaky democratic beginnings. After a brief experiment with democracy, many reverted back to dictatorial rule for a while before finally establishing stable democratic systems on their second or third try. This seems to be not so unusual of a pattern.

The overall growth of democracy in the world, which has been very dramatic not only over the last twenty years but over the last two centuries, has been very much an upward, but not necessarily smooth, curve. There are eighty-five democracies this year; maybe there will only be eighty next year, but there is no reason at all to doubt that this is part of a steady upward trend in the expansion of democracy. There are no exact, hard and fast rules about where and how democracy can come about.

Social science is terribly inexact, and perhaps its most exact pronouncement about democracy in the world is that democracy correlates with affluence. The richer the country, the more likely it is to be democratic, and vice versa. But this is very far from being an absolute correlation. Of the eighty-five countries listed by Freedom House, fully thirty have a per capita GNP of under $2,000. Indeed, seventeen have a per capita GNP of under $1,000.

Similarly, there is a correlation between democracy and a high rate of literacy. But there are any number of countries, including several in Latin America, that now enjoy democratic government and yet have literacy rates that are lower than some of the nondemocratic countries in the world, including a great many of the dictatorships of the Middle East, such as Syria, Iraq, and Libya.

So then, there are no socioeconomic laws or indicators that would lead us to conclude that the Arab world cannot be democratic. What we are left with, then, is the argument about culture; that is, while there is nothing inherent in the physical or economic conditions of this area of the world that would prevent the operation of democracy, it is nonetheless unlikely in this region because the culture of Islam is inhospitable to democracy.

While there may be some truth to this, many other cultures are or have been regarded as inhospitable to democracy yet have undergone a successful transformation to democracy. Samuel Huntington twins Islam with Confucianism as the two large ethical/religious traditions that are regarded as being inhospitable to democracy. Yet we have seen that democracy has been spreading and still is spreading in the Confucian world. One need think of Taiwan, South Korea, and Japan, which is one of the bulwark countries of the democratic world. And yet the skepticism akin to that heard today about the prospects for democracy in the Islamic world was expressed in very similar terms about the prospects for democracy in Japan before it became democratic.

During World War II, when the U.S. government started thinking about what to do with Japan, our leading Japan expert in the State Department, Joseph Grew, who had been our ambassador there, sent President Truman a memo that said, "From the long-range point of view, the best we can hope for is a constitutional monarchy, experience having shown that democracy in Japan would never work."

After we so thoroughly and successfully democratized Japan, one of the great American scholars on Japan, Robert Ward, commented wryly that had General MacArthur and the occupation government known more, they would have accomplished less. If they had really understood Japanese culture, they would have thought it impossible to democratize Japan. Japanese culture would seem to be inherently inhospitable to democracy as it is a culture based on obedience, and hierarchy, and group values, and getting along.

Huntington reminds us—to make the same point in a different direction—that what has been said until recently about Confucianism being inhospitable to democracy was also said a few decades ago about Confucianism and economic growth. And we have certainly seen the wisdom in that.

The relationship between culture and politics is a big, vague and amorphous thing, though no doubt quite important. Specific economic or political outcomes or adaptation to specific economic and political systems are subjects about which we understand very little.

If democracy is both, as I have argued, desirable and reasonable to hope for in the Islamic world, the question naturally arises as to how to bring it about. In order to answer that it is important to first answer the question many ask now: Would democracy in Arab countries be dangerous? In the last few years, Islamist parties have done very well in democratic elections held in several Arab countries, and this has generated a lot of quite justified fear.

There is no easy answer. But while there may be reason to fear the outcome of a single election, and there may be reason to fear a certain militant party's coming to power, there is no reason to fear the institution of true democracy which means not one election for one time only, but a genuine commitment to hold periodic elections.

If a state can achieve democracy, in the sense of elections and free speech that will be followed eventually by more elections, there is not much cause to fear that this or that party that is extreme or irresponsible may win some of the elections, because, in that circumstance, the democratic process itself will have an important moderating effect, as parties, in order to remain in power, are forced to be accountable to the voters, for delivering on their promises, and in the give-and-take of democratic politics.

The thing to fear is the slip between cup and lip; that is, doing things in the name of democracy that do not bring democracy but may simply destabilize an existing government, and replace it with an even worse one. That was exactly the experience we had in the 1970s in Nicaragua and in Iran, where we were pursuing a policy under the rubric of human rights without thinking about the consequences in any given situation.

What we learned is that not all dictatorships are equal, and that sometimes getting rid of one dictatorship results in a worse dictatorship, and that is not progress.

So what needs to be done in trying to foster the growth of democracy in the Islamic world or anyplace else is to differentiate among situations. There are some dictatorial regimes that it is difficult to imagine any alternative being much worse, e.g., Saddam Hussein in Iraq or Moammar Qadhafi in Libya—dictators that are as repressive as any on earth. They are cruel to their own people, have lots of blood on their hands and are very irresponsible in their international actions. While there could be other potential or aspiring dictators in their countries who would be just as obnoxious to us or to the citizens of those countries, it is not likely that there will be worse dictators. So we can afford to be rather free about the question of whether we will destabilize them by promoting democracy.

On the other hand, there are other unelected rulers around the world and in the Middle East, for whom it is easy to imagine worse successors, and, whom we therefore do not want to destabilize. We do want to pressure them for a process of reform and liberalization that will head toward democracy, but this should not be done in a way that will lead to their being overthrown.

And needless to say, while democracy is possible almost everywhere, much more broadly than conventional wisdom has it, in some countries and situations the short-term prospect for democracy is nonetheless much better than in others. And that, too, ought to be a guide to our policy.

Overall, our main task must be to nurture democratic forces in undemocratic countries. This can be accomplished through various means, including the National Endowment for Democracy, radio broadcasting, and political, informational, and aid programs, all of which aim to give encouragement and strength to democratic groups or democratic-minded individuals in countries, in exile, wherever we may find them, so that a democratic future becomes a more realistic prospect when there are changes of regime.

PROMOTING DEMOCRACY AS A PRINCIPLE OF U.S. MIDDLE EAST POLICY

Laurie Mylroie

That the basis for government is properly the will of the people is a widely-held idea in the late twentieth century with intellectual origins in the political philosophy of the seventeenth and eighteenth centuries. The notion that governments properly represent the people was expressed in two forms: the liberals, Hobbes and Locke, emphasized the obligation of governments to protect individual rights, above all the right to life and the right to property. They were writing in reaction, partly, to the religious wars of the seventeenth century.

The idea, as it emerged, was to cause men to concentrate on life in this world and on acquiring material gain so as to make them think less about the life hereafter; the theory was that people occupied with making money would not be so quarrelsome about intangibles. The United States reflects the success of that idea.

Jean Jacques Rousseau, on the other hand, criticized the liberal view and argued that the individualistic pursuit of material gain led to inequalities between men, which, in turn, led to strife, envy and other unpleasant qualities. Rousseau argued that society should be a whole and government should represent the general will.

So there are, in fact, two ways that governments could represent people—by protecting their rights as individuals or by reflecting the general will, the will of the community. That governments should represent their people, or, as Joshua Muravchik has just put it, that people should get what they want, is a nearly universally-held sentiment.

Liberal democracies, like ours, are based on the traditions of Hobbes and Locke. Others, including the former Union of the Soviet Socialist Republics, were based on Rousseau, as modified by Marx and Lenin. It was the claim of the Soviet Union, after all, to represent the bulk of the population, the masses, more effectively than liberal democracy.

Of course, the history of the twentieth century vindicates Hobbes and Locke against Rousseau, Marx, and Lenin, and seems to prove the liberals' emphasis on the need to limit government by protecting individual rights and dividing sovereignty. An important part of the protection of individual rights and division of sovereignty is the separation of political and religious authority. No person or institution possesses a legitimate claim on absolute truth or absolute power.

This does not fit with the Islamic tradition at all because, in Islam, political and religious authority are one. Muhammad was a prophet, a political leader and a military leader all in one. Moreover, sovereignty rests with God or his vice regent, the Prophet and his successors. Traditionally, in Islam, sovereignty does not rest with the people.

So there is a big contradiction between this traditional Muslim view and the modern Western view. Now, we in the West can live with it. We do not feel threatened in our basic values by Islam. Westerners, by and large, are not importing Islamic ways or otherwise acting like Muslims. This contradiction is, however, a problem for Muslims, because they do not feel confident and strong in their tradition.

This, in short, is the root of the Middle East's notorious instability, which makes every other problem so much more difficult to resolve. It is also what makes democracy problematic there. But I am pointing to a very specific feature of traditional Islam and not Islamic culture *per se.*

This is not a complex or difficult argument, nor is it mine alone. Many have made it, but none so eloquently as Bernard Lewis in an essay in the March 23, 1993 *New York Review of Books* entitled, "The Enemies of God." Lewis writes that "It is the seductive appeal of American culture far more than any possible acts by American governments that Islamic fundamentalists see as offering the greatest menace."

Indeed, Muslims have not escaped the influence of the modern notion that sovereignty rests with the people. Like the Union of Soviet Socialist Republics, there are nine Arab republics, including Syria and Iraq. Their claim to rule is that they represent the people, in the Rousseauian sense. Even Iran professes to be a republic, an Islamic republic, representing the first time in history that a Muslim government has claimed popular legitimacy along with religious legitimacy.

But all these so-called "republics" in the Middle East, with the possible exception of Iran, are discredited, particularly after the collapse of the mother of all such republics, the USSR. They are seen by their populations as incompetent, corrupt dictatorships. They have failed to deliver economically; they have failed to fulfill their promise to liberate Palestine and unite the Arabs; and, above all, they have failed to develop societies in which Muslims could feel pride in relation to the West.

Despite the recognized failure of these self-styled republics, there is, with the notable exception of Turkey, no Middle East Muslim government with any plausible claim to be a liberal democracy. Significantly, modern Turkey was founded on the principle of the separation of religious and political authority, in contravention to established Islamic tradition.

The dilemma for Muslims is that, while there has always been a gap between Islam's political theory and its practice, modern times have exacerbated the problems of political legitimacy for Muslim rulers, given the pervasive notion that governments should rule on behalf of their peoples.

This can be illustrated best by looking at Saudi Arabia. The Saudi government, a monarchy, rules in the name of Wahhabism, a strict interpretation of Islam. The political system makes no provision for institutionalized popular representation. Yet the demand is there, reflected in the repeated promises of the Saudi government going back to the 1960s to establish a *shura* or consultative council, the most minimal form of institutionalized political participation. Indeed, after the Gulf War, King Fahd once again promised to create a consultative council. This latest attempt failed to materialize as well.

The Saudi government, unwilling or unable to share political authority, continues to promote a strict Islamic view of the world while claiming to be the guardian of that Islamic way of life.

The Islamic views promoted by the Saudi government do not represent the world *as it is* but as some would like to see it. In this view, Islam is separate and distinct from the West, indeed superior to it and the West is hostile to Islam. That hostility is described by Muslims in terms of the West's actions: American indifference to the Palestinians, the bombing of Iraq, etc. But, as Bernard Lewis has said, the real threat is not Western actions but the seductively corrupting ways of the West, including the demand for political participation.

Even as the Saudi government promotes the idea

that the West is hostile, the country's defense and its wealth, from the sale of its oil, depend on the protection it receives from a non-Muslim power. The West drove out an aggressor and did not itself take the oil that was implicitly threatened had Saddam moved on but returned it to the government of Saudi Arabia.

For much of the Saudi public and government, the U.S. intervention is something to be forgotten and rationalized away. Hence, one finds not a few people saying in Saudi Arabia that the war was an American plot to weaken an Arab nation, that is, Iraq, in order to protect Israel.

The consequence of the Saudi government's inability or unwillingness to share political authority is that it promotes a myth which prevents it from making adequate provisions for its own defense. The way that the Saudi government seeks to maintain its legitimacy is self-defeating and the Saudi impact on the region as it seeks to promote and maintain its legitimacy is not so helpful.

Even as we today are alarmed by the rise of Islamic fundamentalism, particularly in North Africa, we should not forget that it was the government of Saudi Arabia which supported nearly every one of the fundamentalist groups which now threatens the stability of North Africa, including the Islamic Salvation Front (FIS) in Algeria, Hassan al-Turabi in Sudan and the Muslim Brotherhood in Egypt. The Saudis thought that they were gaining leverage by supporting these fundamentalists against secular Arab nationalists.

What if a Middle Eastern government seeks to open up? The problem today is that liberal democrats do not seem to emerge as much as illiberal fundamentalists who may be worse than what in fact exists. Algeria is a case in point. Algeria held elections in December 1991 in which fundamentalists won 189 out of 231 seats in the first round of a two-round election. The Algerian army stepped in to prevent things from going any further. However, these results are misunderstood to a significant degree, because despite the distribution of the seats, the fundamentalists won only 30 percent of the vote. The ruling party, the National Liberation Front (FLN), had concocted a system where it expected to translate a small plurality into a majority. This strategy backfired and the FIS, rather than the FLN, became the beneficiary of this system. The remaining 70 percent of the vote was split among twenty secular parties. A similar distribution of votes has occurred in the parliamentary elections in Jordan in November 1989.

In other words, when given the opportunity to vote, even though a majority of the Arab population does not vote for fundamentalists, a significant minority does. And within that minority that votes for fundamentalists are some who are fervently devoted to that cause. Moreover, the secular vote is divided.

So, one might argue that if the liberalization of authoritarian regimes produces a 30 percent fundamentalist minority, it is perhaps better that strong men should rule the Middle East, i.e., liberalization should yield to stability. But this idea does not work either. Saddam Hussein is a reminder that dictatorial rule is usually unstable. There is a constant tendency to deal with internal problems by externalizing them in aggression.

Gamal Abdul Nasser is another example which is appropriate to recall. After World War II, Egypt faced a more serious threat from Islamic fundamentalism than anything that it has encountered recently. The CIA had some intimation of the plotting of the

Egyptian Free Officers in the early 1950s and, in some respects, welcomed the 1952 coup.

The idea at the time was that the military could be a modernizing force in the Arab world that would get rid of corrupt dictatorships and deal more effectively with reactionary threats like Islamic fundamentalism. But it did not work that way. Initially, the coup was not popular in Egypt; only when Nasser began to adopt the same anti-Westernism as the fundamentalists did he become an Arab hero.

An Egyptian friend once explained this to me in terms of his personal experience. When Nasser took over, he at first did not like Nasser because he had promised democracy but did not follow through on this promise. But when Nasser nationalized the Suez Canal, little Egypt stood up to Great Britain, which had ruled it for a century, and he felt so happy and excited that he forgot all about democracy.

Like Joshua Muravchik, I believe that nothing but the establishment of liberal democracy in the Middle East will bring peace and stability to the region. But it is not an easy project; maybe it is not even possible. But there are ways in which it can be pursued without undue risk of making the situation worse than it is.

First, it is important to differentiate among Middle Eastern states and peoples. Populations of different countries in the Middle East have different interests, a fact that can be hidden by the promiscuous use of phrases such as "Arab world" and "Muslim world." There are Arab countries and Arab peoples. In those countries, whose populations have suffered grievous pain because of the excesses of anti-Western ideology (an ideology shared by both Islamic fundamentalists and Arab nationalists like Nasser), the attitudes of the various populations are different.

Both Kuwait and Iraq certainly fall into this category. Kuwait restored its national assembly and held elections last year. Those elections did not produce a bunch of fanatics; rather, the national assembly is a reasonably sober body and it is breaking many ideological tenets that usually compromise Western relations with Arab states. Above all, Kuwaitis increasingly define their interests using Western catch phrases and ideology.

For example, a fundamentalist member of parliament recently suggested that Kuwait should establish an Islamic guidance body. In response, several Kuwaiti papers averred that such a body was unnecessary as it would limit personal freedoms, and that Kuwait had more urgent problems to deal with, like economic reconstruction. This response is indicative of a new approach on the part of the Kuwaiti press. Typically, public Arab discourse is very delicate in its coverage of issues related to Islam or Arab nationalism, and direct refutation of their desirability is unusual.

Iraq is another example of a population which has been so abused by the excesses of a fundamentalist or nationalist ideology that may provide fertile ground for responsible self-government. Indeed, the complaint of the Iraqi population regarding the Gulf War was not that the United States attacked Iraq but that it left Saddam in power. The idea that a population would welcome a war against its own government was so foreign to the way many Americans imagined Arab politics, or Iraqi politics, and the way other Arabs described Iraq that the Western media was, in fact, very slow to report accurately the general Iraqi perception: "The war is fine, just get rid of Saddam for us."

One of the few Arab communities in which there is a free-ranging political debate, where prominent figures speak the language of liberal democracy, shorn of the anti-Western sentiment or the uneasy relations with the West that characterizes many Arab intellectuals, is the Iraqi exile community. For that, many outspoken individuals have been brutally criticized by other Arabs, particularly by Palestinians, as traitors and agents.

The mainstream Iraqi opposition, the Iraqi National Congress, maintains a neutral position on the ideological issues which usually divide the West from the Arab countries, including the Palestinian question. This is a reflection of the extremity of the repression in Iraq and a willingness to abandon the ideologies which other Arab populations seem committed to.

This phenomenon is particularly evident among Iraq's Kurds, who held elections in May 1992, without violence. The Kurdish elections were the freest elections ever held in Iraq, indeed the freest elections held in an Arab country in recent times. On the surface, there was nothing in the experience of the Kurds, a tribal people who had never known freedom, to suggest that they were capable of such a thing. I suppose a cultural argument about the Kurds would say they could not democratize with no prior experience.

But, upon reflection, there were reasons for the success of the Kurds' democratic experiment. They include a very deep revulsion against dictatorship because of the genocidal repression they suffered at the hands of a brutal dictator and also a sense that democracy was somehow the only form of civilized government.

In principle, the West should be promoting democracy and human rights in the Middle East, because ultimately that is the only way that the region will know peace and stability. That principle could probably be held in abeyance where the effort to promote it would lead to regimes that are more repressive than those that exist now. That does not mean abandoning the principle. Furthermore, there are places in the Middle East where it is appropriate to promote democracy. And, finally, one of the more effective tools that the West has against Islamic fundamentalist countries that seek to export their fundamentalism and their terror is precisely an emphasis on human rights and democracy. The West should stress that the treatment of the sizable majority of their populations that do not necessarily go along with the government and its policies by the governments of Iran and Sudan will not be tolerated.

A PHASED INTRODUCTION OF ISLAMISTS

Graham Fuller

There is little virtue in holding Jesuitical debates about whether Islam is compatible with democracy. The same discussions might apply to Judaism or Christianity, and they have been debated for centuries. The real issue is how Muslims are going to think about democracy. And it is very difficult to think that, *a priori*, most Muslims are going to say, "No, we prefer not to have democracy."

The issue is, how are Muslims, as members of their society, going to deal with democracy? What are Muslims' aspirations? How do they want to live and under what kinds of government and rule? What do they want done to them by regimes?

I do not think there is a consensus on the part of Muslims for the abolition of freedoms that might be granted to them. It is clear, furthermore, that many Muslims who believe there is a role for Islam in politics do not agree with all Islamists and radicals. So, here again, in talking about what Muslims want, there is a considerable spectrum of opinion that needs to be kept in mind.

I believe the entry of Islam in some form into Middle Eastern politics is inevitable for several reasons.

First of all, and most worrisome, the status quo in most countries of the Middle East now is unacceptable, unstable and illegitimate in terms of the kinds of governments that currently rule. Governments are under tremendous assault from all quarters, with economic desperation being fueled by very high population growth rates, huge needs to import food and vast under- and unemployment.

And, politically, many governments are not able

to meet the demands of the people. They are finding it increasingly difficult to repress the people in order to stay in power, yet seem to be unwilling to broaden the basis of rule or bring more people into the government—even to share the blame. And "sharing the blame" is often one of the basic means by which democracies come into being.

Given this disastrous status quo, I am afraid that something is going to give, and fairly soon, in many countries of the Middle East where regimes are simply not able to meet the needs of the people or the country.

Unfortunately, Islamists are best poised, of all political groups in the region, to take advantage of this situation. The tragedy is that there are few political alternatives. It need not necessarily be that way, but given how governments are now constructed in the Middle East, few plausible, viable opposition parties have been allowed to gather strength and present themselves as real alternatives to the Islamists. So this is another reason why Islam will inevitably become part of the political process.

It is furthermore impossible to think that, in societies where Islam is the basic religion, it will not enter into the political discourse. Religion enters into the Christian and Jewish discourse, both in the United States, a country which has ostensibly gone far toward the separation of church and state, in Israel and elsewhere. The question is how and in what way will Islam enter into the political discourse in the Middle East.

Islam is also a nativist tradition in a region thirsting for some kind of legitimate nativist roots for its own political philosophy. I am not saying Islam has to be anti-Western or it has to be totally different than the West, but it is reassuring to Muslims when political theory has some kind of

Islamic basis.

It must be remembered, too, that Islam is not homogeneous. It is very dangerous to think of Islam as simply being one movement. There are many different groups, even within the Islamists, who disagree strongly among themselves.

It should be noted parenthetically that there are even some modernizing aspects to Islamism. Ironically, Islamist movements are bringing women into the political system in many countries, such as Iran, North Africa, and elsewhere. Islamists are regularly joined by secular opposition forces, for instance. At one point in Algeria, they marched virtually in lockstep against government policy.

The Islamist movements are likewise serving to politicize and mobilize elements of the population in states where this has never happened before. One may regret that the Islamists are almost the only ones carrying out this mobilization process, but they are doing it, and the mobilization and politicization of populations is an essential stage in societies' gradual movement towards democratization.

Many Islamists are actually critiquing existing governments on the basis of absence of human rights and democratic instruments. This may seem to some to be just a cynical move to exploit liberal principles to gain power, only to abolish them once in power. Some may undoubtedly want to do that; others do not. But the fact is, Islamists are compelled to base their critique of existing regimes on many of the liberal grounds that we ourselves would use to criticize regimes.

A critical point is that Islamism, once it enters the political system will surely weaken over time, for a number of reasons. First, Islamism does not have many unique answers to problems. Islamists may come up with some interesting thoughts, or some useful approaches in certain areas, but Islam does not have any unique answers. Yet the longer Islamists are excluded from the system, the more they are able to maintain that Islam is the only answer. Let them prove whether they have the answers. Let them demonstrate that they have a particular approach. I submit that they do not have the answers and that ultimately this point will be demonstrated. Their interpretations are contested, even by many Muslims within their own ranks. There is no Islamist unity that will be able to be maintained throughout that period.

Islamism has the allure of the untried; once tried in politics, however, much of that allure will disappear. In Turkey, Islamists generally get 12 to 15 percent of the vote since having been allowed into politics. In Pakistan, they have never done much better than 12 to 15 percent in elections. In Iran, today or tomorrow or ten years from now, if genuinely free elections are held there, it is unlikely that many people will get excited at the idea of voting for an Islamist party after the experience of the Islamic Republic. One would not wish upon every nation the need to go through an Islamist experience to find that out, but I think the experience of Islam in politics, even to a limited extent, will lessen its momentum and appeal.

Islamism is now in the process of becoming a movement and not just a political party. Movements as such tend to be stronger, more emotive and more appealing in many respects. Political parties, on the other hand, have to come up with cold, hard answers to life's problems.

Women, increasingly, will grow hostile to Islamist movements, if the latter are intent on keeping women isolated and out of political power and out of the job market in the future.

Islamists will inevitably be forced to compromise with political reality as they move into positions of authority within parliaments and have to deal with those they do not agree with. When Islamism is in power, there will be winners and losers, according to the reforms and changes made. They will make enemies.

Islamists are already forced to talk in terms of the Universal Declaration of Human Rights and justify why they are not fully supporting democratic principles, for example, in Sudan, Iran or even Pakistan. They have had to apologize on those grounds and find justifications to explain why there are variations. In other words, the basis for the liberal democratic argument is already largely accepted. The terms of the liberal dialogue have in many cases been implicitly accepted, even if not explicitly.

There are, of course, many negative features to Islamism coming to power. I do not, in fact, advocate its coming to power. But this is going to happen in many states, in one fashion or another; the question is, how do we manage the process in order to limit any possible negative repercussions.

There are many negative features to political Islam. There are criminal aspects to many of the Islamic extremist organizations, of which in Egypt we see some particularly vicious examples, including assassinations, murders, bombings—criminal acts that must be punished appropriately.

Secondly, some Islamists have ideologically totalitarian visions, but they are essentially part of a small minority. The issue is how to prevent these violent minorities from gaining total control over Islamist movements and imposing totalitarian ideas.

Certainly, another negative feature is that the most prominent example of an Islamist government in power, Iran, has so far not been encouraging. But Iran is evolving very quickly, even if the most radical of the Islamist elements control the "export of Islam," a disruptive element of Iranian policy. But that aside, processes in Iran are slowly moving in the direction of de-Islamizing the state in critical respects, as pragmatism gains ground in many other areas, including a remarkably open parliament.

Iran possesses a poor human rights record and certainly a conservative social agenda under which most of us would not want to live. But these issues are the subject of legitimate debate among the Islamists.

As democracy comes to the Middle East, it is going to be almost universally destabilizing, at least initially. We have to recognize this. The minorities that now run Bahrain, Iraq and Syria will no longer be running those states. Other states that are ruled by majorities in which minorities are repressed will find those minorities having a much greater voice.

There will be increasing social change. Old elites that have been holding onto power will lose out, and the process will surely be destabilizing. But what is the alternative? During the Cold War, one could argue that destabilization worked in the interest of the Soviets. That excuse is gone today.

We must navigate the process by which governments eventually achieve the kind of stabilization of political forces that occurs when governments reflect the rough proportionality of forces within society. The process is not going to be easy, and it may have unpleasant and negative consequences. We must get through this process if we are to ever arrive at that state of more democratic governance that is the sole, long-term guarantee of moderate and more stable politics free from the uncontrolled whims of dictatorial rule.

Ultimately, the mechanics of how this happens is all important. It will happen. But how it happens is critical. When Islamists emerge from a state of utter repression and explode into some democratic victory, this sudden release of forces represents the single most negative and undesirable manner Islam can enter the political process.

The clearest model of this phenomenon is, of course, Iran. Algeria could have moved in that direction as well. We should hope to see Islamic forces gradually enter the political system—and not because we want them or like them, but because they will inevitably enter under some guise or other. Let them take over cities and municipalities, as they have in Algeria. Let people see how the cities they run experience serious problems. Let them come gradually into parliaments. Phased introduction, in other words, is a very critical point.

In future elections, states should agree in advance on compacts of behavior, such that political parties who contest for power will agree not to later abolish the democratic process. Of course, compacts cannot provide an absolute guarantee. Islamists can sign any piece of paper they want, then come to power and abolish the system. But the greater the restraints and the greater the advance agreements on the rules of the game, the harder it will be to delegitimize the system.

But inevitably, there is going to be some movement backwards as well as forwards. Turkey has taken at least three attempts—three coups—to get democracy on track, but now it is not looking too bad. There may even be a fourth setback in Turkey, but Turks are beginning to get used to the democratic process. This will, in time, happen elsewhere.

There are thresholds by which fringe groups can be kept out, by establishing, for example, that parties must obtain a minimum of 3 to 4 percent of the vote to be represented in parliament, etc. These mechanical aspects of democracy are very important. Israel itself knows that threshold election laws can have a critical impact on the governability or the nongovernability even of democracies. An electoral structure of "winner take all" versus other kinds of representational systems is very critical to how Islamists will do in some of these elections.

Rather than just one Islamist party, I would like to see a multiplicity of Islamic parties, with natural disagreements among them. Let more of them come out. Let one hundred flowers bloom so that they will oppose each other, so that there will be debate. One of the biggest problems within Islamic society so far is that there has not been honest critique of the shortcomings and weaknesses of other Islamic movements. Islamists have been very coy and unwilling to talk about these sensitive issues, especially when they are out of power, because they feel this quest for solidarity.

I believe that there will be a growth in Islamic forces. It is regrettable that, at this point, they are the only opposition forces that exist. Many states that now face election pressures must make it their business, urgently, to assure that other opposition parties emerge, apart from the Islamists.

One basic, negative feature of the Islamists that is very disturbing is their fundamental anti-Westernism. The degree of anti-Westernism that will remain within these systems will depend critically on the character of international politics. If the West, and the United States in particular, uses democracy as a means to attack our enemies, but overlooks democratic criterion when it comes to our friends, then Muslims will be convinced that the democratic rhetoric that is coming from the West is just the latest Western idea about how to dominate the Middle East.

If the West does seem to apply questions of principle equitably, if there are no double standards and if we see a general diminution of Western efforts to dominate the Middle East, in one respect or another, then our values will be accepted more readily and less cynically than they have been to date.

Surely, illegitimate regimes all over the entire Middle East are now very much against the ropes. We have to figure out how we are going to get through the process of liberalization and democratization, while simultaneously managing the process of Islam entering the political system.

If there is no liberalization because of our fear of Islam, then we will simply build towards greater political and social explosion with worse consequences for all. This is the supreme challenge of the next several decades as we seek to change the very political groundwork in the Middle East that has brought forth the likes of Saddam Hussein. There has to be a better way for politics to be conducted in the Middle East, and Muslims know it. After all, they have been the chief victims in the past.

WHERE ISLAM AND DEMOCRACY
PART WAYS

Martin Kramer

My purpose is to consider and critique the argument which has emerged as conventional wisdom about Islamic fundamentalism, and which has been echoed here in the presentation by Graham Fuller, that is that Islamic fundamentalist movements are, in reality, democracy movements and reform movements in disguise.

Graham did make the case, most eloquently, and perhaps a bit extravagantly, in the piece he wrote on Islamic fundamentalism for the *Washington Post* last year, when he called it "a movement that is historically inevitable and politically 'tamable.' Over the long run, it even represents ultimate political progress toward greater democracy and popular government."[1]

Robin Wright has made a parallel argument, in which she declared Islam to be "at a juncture increasingly equated with the Protestant Reformation," thanks to the growing number of fundamentalists who "are now trying to reconcile moral and religious tenets with modern life, political competition and free markets."[2]

This representation of Islamic fundamentalism, which has gained widespread currency in academic and journalistic circles, is being driven simultaneously by two different rationales. The first is a variation of democracy theory, largely the

---

1 Graham Fuller, "Islamic Fundamentalism: No Long-Term Threat," *Washington Post*, January 13, 1992.
2 Robin Wright, "Islam, Democracy, and the West," *Foreign Affairs*, Vol. 71, No. 3, Summer 1992.

province of political scientists; the second is a tendency towards Islamic apologetics, which is evident among some Western students of Islam. I submit that their shared conclusion, that Islamic fundamentalism is really not fundamentalism at all but an earnest yearning for democracy and reform in Islamic guise, is driven more by disciplinary commitments and biases than by the evidence.

This variation of democracy theory, first of all, is committed to a thesis that the world is moving steadily and inexorably towards democratization in a universal and inevitable process. The Islamic Arab world is no exception. But there is a difficulty in the case of the Arab world because there are no obvious democracy movements, movements with which Western opinion would immediately sympathize, as there are in Eastern Europe.

Nonetheless, these are immensely popular and populist movements, Islamic in nature, and they demand free elections and the "rule of law." Since theory posits that democracy movements must be emerging here as elsewhere, and since the only movements that seem to be thriving are Islamic, logic strongly suggests that Islamic movements may well be democracy movements in disguise.

To be sure, much that they actually say and do is troubling. They talk about Islamic government rather than democracy; Bernard Lewis is right when he writes that fundamentalists do not use or even misuse the term "democracy" in their discourse.[1] And their notion of the "rule of law" refers to the unalterable law of Islam.

Nevertheless, the argument goes, this is a different cultural setting. If we cannot see the

---

[1]   Bernard Lewis, "Islam and Liberal Democracy," *The Atlantic Monthly*, February 1993.

democratic yearning beneath the surface, then perhaps it is a narrowness of our own vision and the result of our Western biases.

Some Western students of Islam are equally committed. They have invested immense energies in trying to bring about a Western understanding of Islam, an understanding that has always been sorely lacking. They are quite right that Islam, as a system of beliefs that comforts and inspires hundreds of millions of people, has not always gotten its due in the West, certainly not in the media. And one does find in the West, a lamentable tendency to associate the religion of Islam with terror and despotism.

These students of Islam find themselves in the awkward position of being asked about Islam only when someone is assassinated or something is blown up. They have been more than justified in reminding the world on these occasions that Islam is not Islamic fundamentalism.

But, recently, they have begun to realize that in many places, Islamic fundamentalism is becoming normative Islam. This is not the Islam that they had been defending. They had assumed that Islam was moving in another direction, towards Islamic modernism, the attempt to reconcile Islam with modern values.

In point of fact, Islamic modernism has been in eclipse for some time, yet the basic assumption of many scholars remains that the mainstream of Islamic thought must move, inevitably, again, towards some sort of enlightened reform. And if this is so, then the burgeoning fundamentalist movements cannot be what they seem to be, that is, an atavistic regression. Beneath their rough exterior, then, the work of reform must be underway. And if we cannot see this clearly, it is because of Western prejudice against Islam.

As you will have noted, a similar determinism has led both the democracy theorists and the students of Islam to their conclusions about Islamic fundamentalism. And these conclusions, I submit, are basically ideological. Not surprisingly, they fly straight in the face of an overwhelming amount of evidence, both of fundamentalist thought and practice.[1]

Several salient issues need to be addressed. First, are the fundamentalists attempting to reconcile Islam with democracy? Are they indeed formulating their thought within the confines of the democratic discourse, as defined in the preceding presentations?

I see no evidence for this. Indeed, it seems that the principled position of every major fundamentalist thinker, the authors of the source texts that fundamentalists read, from Casablanca to Kabul, is that democracy is irrelevant to Islam and that Islam is superior to democracy. In this view, the fatal flaw of democracy is that it rests upon the sovereignty of the people. In Islam, God is sovereign, and his will is expressed in the *sharia*, the divinely revealed law of Islam. Democracy, which places the prerogative of legislation in the hands of the people, is the very essence of arbitrary government, because it turns on the whim of a shifting electorate, and electorates always shift, by their nature. No fundamentalist is prepared to submit to the will of that electorate, if it defies Islamic law. As Algeria's most outspoken fundamentalist put it, "One does not vote for God. One obeys him."

There are those in these movements today who allow that believers may participate in elections, envisioned as a kind of referendum of allegiance to a

---

[1] See Martin Kramer, "Islam vs. Democracy," *Commentary*, January 1993.

regime of divine justice, which would eventually bring Islam to power. But once established in power, the fundamentalists would be remiss in their Islamic obligation were they to let it slip from their hands. A nomocracy of Islamic law cannot envision its own disestablishment.

This does not mean that there can be no debate about the implementation of Islamic law where the law is vague, but there can be no debate over the primacy of the law itself, especially on points where it is not vague: the duties and punishments it imposes, and its principled inequalities between Muslims and non-Muslims, and men and women.

Nor can the debate take the freewheeling form often associated with democracy, with the formation of parties or individual campaigning. The fundamentalist revulsion against party conflict and personalities in democratic politics was best expressed by Dr. Hassan al-Turabi, himself armed with law degrees from the University of London and the Sorbonne, whose tract on the Islamic state argues that such a state has no need of party politics or political campaigns.

While Islamic law does not expressly forbid a multi-party system, he has written that "This is a form of factionalism that can be very oppressive of individual freedom and divisive of the community, and it is therefore antithetical to a Muslim's ultimate responsibility to God."

As for campaigning, he goes on to say that "In Islam, no one is entitled to conduct a campaign for themselves, directly or indirectly, in the manner of a Western electoral campaign. The presentation of candidates would be entrusted to a neutral institution that would explain to the people the options offered in policies and personalities."

I think we all recognize this formula of elections

without parties or candidates for what it is. It is a tacit justification of one-party rule, such as that over which Dr. Turabi currently presides in the Sudan.

But surely there must be significant differences among Islamic fundamentalists on these points? After all, note the doubters, the Arab Muslim world covers a vast expanse. There are many different movements which go by many different names. Perhaps it is possible to sort the moderates from the radicals and encourage the process of moderation in these movements.

Now it is, of course, quite obvious that circumstances do differ across the expanse of Islam. No two situations are identical. No two fundamentalist movements are identical. In the past, such movements often functioned in isolation. But the world is a changing place, and so is the Islamic world.

Just as modern technology has wired fundamentalism in this country (the televangelists come readily to mind), so it is now wiring Islamic fundamentalism. The jet, the fax, and the cassette have created global villages of Islamic fundamentalism. I say "villages" and not "village" because there are several of them. Perhaps the most important are that of the Muslim Brotherhood and that of the Islamic Republic of Iran. But each of these villages stretches from one end of the Muslim world to the other, and, at some crucial points, they even overlap.

In these villages, ideas and people move rapidly. Movements learn from, imitate, and often assist one another. The international Islamic *jihad* against the Soviet occupation of Afghanistan was one of their great achievements, a moral equivalent of the Spanish Civil War, which drew men and materiel from throughout Islam in a way that would have been unthinkable only a decade before. And the phenomenon of Hezbollah in Lebanon cannot be understood without reference to its place in the closely-linked network that revolves around Iran.

Today these global villages are indeed global, extending even into the great cities of the West, as recent events have demonstrated quite vividly. In short, no Islamic fundamentalist movement can be regarded *sui generis*. No fundamentalist organization exists in a vacuum. In this interconnected world, there is no sealed laboratory in which a fundamentalist experiment can be conducted. Fundamentalism's fortunes in Algeria, for example, will affect the entirety of North Africa and much of the Middle East in ways that will be difficult to predict, but affect they will.

Maybe so, one might ask, but why should all this affect Western interests adversely? After all, states which have sold oil will continue to sell it. States which have needed aid, will continue to need it, even if they come under fundamentalist rule. Once in power, argues John Esposito, fundamentalists will "generally operate on the basis of national interests and demonstrate a flexibility that reflects acceptance of the realities of a globally interdependent world."[1] Once enmeshed in the world of real politics, the fundamentalists will have to accommodate it.

The argument has also been made, in the specific American context, that the Sunni fundamentalist movements did work with Pakistan, Saudi Arabia and even the U.S. in promoting the *jihad* against the Soviet occupation of Afghanistan. This is sometimes introduced as evidence that they are not anti-Western or are even prepared to work with the

---

[1] John Esposito, *The Islamic Threat: Myth or Reality* (New York: Oxford University Press, 1992).

West.

The argument, here again, seems to me very thin. Even in the promotion of the Afghan *jihad*, the fundamentalists never saw themselves as partners of the West in the Cold War. They realized that the West, for its own reasons, was prepared to arm them for their *jihad*, but, in their view, they were acting solely for the purpose of creating an Islamic Afghanistan. No doubt, were the U.S. prepared to sell them even more guns to create even more Islamic states, they would deal happily with it. But, ultimately, the idea would be to turn all these guns and states into the basis for Islam's emergence into great power status.

The fundamentalists do not speak in terms of a globally interdependent world. They now fantasize about a new world order very different from the one imagined in the West. In their vision, Islam will indeed sell its oil, provided Muslims would be allowed to invest the proceeds in instruments of war to enable them to reverse the course of modern history. This proliferation will eventually create a new world order based not on American hegemony but on a new balance of power between a reawakened Islam and the West.

As Hezbollah's mentor, Sayyid Fadlallah, has put it, "We may not have the actual power the U.S. has, but we had the power previously and we now have the foundations to develop that power in the future."

From the fundamentalist point of view, the restored balance between Islam and the West excludes the intrusive existence of Israel in the lands of Islam. Fundamentalists are uncompromisingly theological in their understanding of the Arab-Israeli conflict. You no have doubt heard the Hamas covenant recited to you chapter and verse now, *ad nauseam.* I would only suggest, though, that it be kept in mind that this happens to be a living covenant, unlike those of some other organizations.

In the fundamentalist view, Palestine is a land sacred to Islam; it is a land stolen by the Jews. Israel is a cancer in the Islamic world, planted by Western imperialism and nurtured by the United States. This is the general view held by all these movements, from the Shi'ite movements that receive guidance and support from Iran to the Sunni movements in the Muslim Brotherhood tradition.

Fundamentalist opposition to the American-sponsored Arab-Israeli peace process has been unequivocal and often violent, and I defy anyone to find a silver lining in the fundamentalist position.

In sum, the hopes placed on these fundamentalist movements by Western intellectuals have been misplaced in the way that so many Western intellectuals have misplaced their hopes before. Whether the rationale is democracy theory, apologetics for Islam or garden variety Third Worldism, the basic argument is the same: Ignore what the fundamentalists say to one another, ignore what they do to others. They must inevitably become what we need them to be. And the quicker we give in to them, the sooner that will happen.

Frankly, I confess I have moments when I wish this were true. However, the fundamentalists themselves have countered each of the arguments made on their behalf. I find them persuasive and they have raised more than reasonable doubt about the wisdom which has become so conventional this past year.

My purpose here has not been to prescribe specific policies for particular governments but to note some simple truths about Islamism. But the debate over what should be done has to be prefaced by a hard look at what is and a return to the careful reading of the sources. If you wish, call this fundamentalism.

ISLAM, DEMOCRACY, AND THE CHALLENGE OF POLITICAL CHANGE

Mohammed Abdelbeki Hermassi

Ten years ago, many people wondered whether it would be possible for Muslim countries to have, in the age of the nation-state, the equivalent of a European Christian Democrat party.

This question was very seriously debated by many political scientists, sociologists and journalists. In terms of strict intellectual debate, the response was not very encouraging for two reasons. First of all, because the Christian Democrat parties in Europe appeared after a set of processes had first taken place: the formation of nation-states, political parties and unions, including parties that had decided to exclude religion from political affairs. Most Christian Democratic parties have entered the political process as a component of a larger system. They have accepted the removal of the church from secular affairs, though maintaining the right to draw on religious values. This has not been the case of most Islamist movements, whose blueprints exclude most of what has been accumulated historically in their country and elsewhere.

The second reason that led us to be a little bit more pessimistic was the fact that Christianity went through the Reformation. Christianity faced challenges that led it to revise its principles and its basic positions on life and politics. In the Muslim world, there has been no equivalent period of reform. The occupation of Islamic lands by colonial and imperial powers has led Islam to do what it does best; that is, to oppose, but not to really reform itself or modernize.

Thus, today we find ourselves discussing the

Islamization of modernity, while rarely do we raise the question of the modernization of Islam.

But, in the last few years, this debate has somehow disappeared, partly because it was settled in practical terms. How? The idea of incorporating and recognizing a Muslim party has ceased, because the basis for that idea has disappeared. To incorporate an Islamist party into the body politic would require the existence of a moderate form of Islamism, one capable of debating issues, making compromises, allowing participation in elections and accepting, or at least tolerating, groups other than themselves.

What is obvious today is the radicalization of the Islamic movement. After the killing of political officials, security personnel and tourists, after the attacks on non-Muslim minorities, after the bombing of public places, it is obvious that we cannot talk about a moderate Islamism anymore, for the concept of moderate Islamism is practically dead.

The generation of political leaders who tried to give elections a chance and tried to play the political game legally have been replaced. This new generation of leaders is often a terrorist apparatus, not very different from the Red Army, the Red Brigade, Action Directe and other terrorist groups which appeared in Europe in the 1970s after the breakdown of what the Left had represented in Europe.

Even Egypt, which for many years set the pattern for other Arab countries, has had to revise its own approach. For many years, Egypt's Islamists were divided between those who were cooptable, able to be taken, through different devices, into the parliament and into the political life of the country, and those who are noncooptable, like Jihad and Jama'at, who were pushed to the margin and, at times, repressed.

This distinction cannot be drawn anymore,

because the young men from Jihad and from Jama'at, are, when pursued in the rural areas, received by the young followers of the Muslim Brotherhood. So the model of trying to coopt those moderates and reject intransigent Islamists no longer works.

Actually, the whole philosophy and attitude toward violence has changed. In the 1930s, when the Muslim Brotherhood first became politically active under the leadership of Hassan al-Banna, the use of violence was rare, though there are some prominent examples such as the murder of Boutros Boutros-Ghali's father. There were, to be sure, already frightening occurrences, but these were exceptions.

What has changed is that violence, formerly an exception, is now used as a method and as a strategy to get power. This changes everything. Today, Tunisia, not Egypt, is setting the trend by saying that politics and religion do not mix, and that no party should ever be allowed to exist if it is based on a religious, ethnic or other primordial basis. I am not saying this because I am Tunisian; I am saying this because this is what the Algerians are saying, and this is what Egyptian President Hosni Mubarak himself has said.

Almost all Arab governments have come to the same conclusion, i.e., that no government is really safe from Islamist radicalism, which has become increasingly a threat to political order. This is the case in Algeria, Tunisia and Egypt, as well as in the Gulf countries, which have entirely re-evaluated their attitude since the Gulf War. Having sided with Baghdad, the Islamists lost their subsidies, and now, for the first time, Saudi Arabia, a country that has traditionally supported fundamentalism, is expressing opposition to the use of mosques in politics.

Actually, the Islamist challenge is leading almost

all Arab governments, for the first time, to agree on certain basic things. Last January, the interior ministers from the Arab states met in Tunis and agreed on a set of principles. One such principle is that no Arab country is safe from extremism. They also agreed on the principle of extradition of terrorists.

I believe that it is not only the Islamists who have changed. I think the Arab governments have taken part in this change, and that the big powers have reached similar conclusions.

France's discussions of these issues—with which I am more familiar than the debate in the United States—are illustrative of European thinking on the whole. In France there were two schools of thought with respect to Islamism and particularly the Algerian situation.

The first camp, which I call "the cynical *laissez-faire*," avers that the Islamists may come to power, particularly in Algeria, but once they are there, the laws of politics will take their own course. The Islamists will expose their own inability to govern, devise economic and social policies, and would fail to bring anything different from what is prevailing. In other words, regimes should allow the Islamists to come to power because, once there, the inadequacies of their solutions will become readily observable and the popularity of the Islamists will thus wane.

The camp that finally prevailed in France, however, argues that if the Islamists were to gain power in Algeria, they would certainly seek to spread their influence, setting off a "domino effect" throughout North Africa and have a very negative effect in the whole Mediterranean area. Security experts, in particular, were extremely frightened by what may happen in France itself because of the presence of millions of Algerians there.

This fear is just one illustration why France, in the end, chose to support the existing government in Algeria, despite their differences. France would rather support its *bête noire* than permit the establishment of fundamentalist rule in the Maghreb.

With respect to the Arab-Israeli peace process, I think it is fair to say that all the Arab governments are now involved in one way or another and have adapted themselves to the idea of this process. In the Arab world, the notion of a new world order, which appeared with the aftermath of the Cold War, is taken very seriously.

No Arab government wants to be left out of this emerging new world order. No Arab government now is left to oppose the Camp David process, as it is called. There is no more "rejectionist front." I submit to you that the Islamists, helped by Iran and Sudan, perceive themselves as the last rampart of rejectionism and steadfastness. And that, I think, is important for the area and for the peace process as well.

We have moved from Islamism as a moderate political formation to Islamism as a new form of attempted terrorist takeover. The Islamist protest has drifted into fundamentalist violence and that, in turn, has led various governments to adopt a policy of exclusion and crackdown.

Does this seriously endanger the prospects of democratization in the region? It certainly does. If the situation remains as it is—we will see what it is called in French, *le tout subversif contre le tout repressif*—all-out repression against all-out subversion. This would be a catastrophe for all.

Usually, this problem is thought of as a dichotomy between the strictly security-based approach to Islamism and the political approach. Many advocate political openness, overtures to the Islamists, increased democratization, the integration of the Islamists, giving them a political party and devising a scheme for power-sharing. That would have been fine had it happened twelve or fifteen years ago. But in view of the violent radicalization of Islamism, this political approach is a little bit too late. It is anachronistic.

The Islamists' drift toward violence is easily observable in their public statements and actions. In Tunisia, for instance, Rashid Ghannouchi has for many years adopted a Jeffersonian tone. Recently, he said, "For a while we have been looking for a stall in the *souk*. Well, we did not receive it, that could not be, and now we want the whole *souk*."

The arguments themselves have changed. Formerly, the Islamists described themselves as one part of the political puzzle. In the last few years, however, they have started saying that they are the party of the majority. I would argue that, to the extent that single parties have lost their legitimacy, there is absolutely no room to replace one national party with one religious party.

At any rate, with this radicalization of the Islamists, I believe that the first scenario of incorporation is, as I said, inadequate and naive.

On the other hand, democratization does not depend on an instantaneous decision, as if a good, enlightened despot could turn into a democrat. Democracy is, as we all know, a long-term process that requires foundations. Such foundations are still to be established in the Middle East. But, I think, we are entitled to start the first step, to provide the preconditions and the foundations for democracy. A different approach, a political/developmental approach, needs to be followed.

In order to face the Islamist challenge and open up

the political system, we have to both strengthen and consolidate political openness and, at the same time, try to improve the daily living conditions of the population.

The first political step in facing the Islamists in terms of democratization, is the development of a credible opposition.

The FIS may have won the Algerian elections in December 1991 and January 1992, but it did not win because it enjoys a monopoly on the population's support. As many observers have pointed out, only 25 percent of the eligible voters voted for the FIS—its victory was by default. It won because the FLN became terribly weak and discredited and never wanted to strengthen the various opposition parties.

In Egypt and Tunisia, the ruling parties have been strong. This is why each time there are free elections, the ruling parties win. But this is not enough; there have to be credible opposition parties.

One might think that most incumbent rulers are not going to develop a credible opposition easily. But this has been done in Turkey and in Mexico. And in Tunisia, the laws have lately been changed to guarantee political parties access to parliament.

Another element of this political openness, is to allow freedom of the press. We should also emphasize an independent judiciary and, particularly, while waiting for full democratization, accord respect to the leagues of human rights in the Arab world. Indeed, leagues of human rights are important, not only on humanist grounds, but on political grounds.

In his recent book on human rights in the Arab world, Kevin Dwyer, a leader of a human rights league, said that:

You know the league in our country is not the equivalent of a human rights league in France or the United States. In those democratic countries, political parties fill the political stage and the human rights organizations are marginal. They busy themselves with particular cases of individuals whose rights have been violated. But here, because freedoms are so weak, because the parties are so weak, they do not fill the political stage, [and] the league is called to play a central role.[1]

Now, when the unions, the Islamists or any other parties are attacked, everyone turns to the league and wants to know what the league's position is, such that the league is pushed into a role that is much more important than what its fundamental role should be.

There is another reason to emphasize the role of leagues of human rights in Egypt, Tunisia and Algeria. In the absence of full debate, and given the weakness of the older political parties, these leagues represent the whole spectrum of opinion. In all three countries, the leagues have included people from left to right; there are Arabs, Jews, Berbers and Copts— the whole political spectrum and the whole ethnic spectrum are truly represented. Human rights leagues are the only forum that is both representative and where debate is conducted in as democratic a manner as possible. This, then, is the political component of my approach.

The other component is development. Arab societies are in general bifurcated; they are divided right down the middle between those who are in and those who are out, those who are included in the

---

1   Kevin Dwyer, *Arab Voices: The Human Rights Debate in the Middle East* (Berkeley: University of California Press, 1991).

modern, world-class economy, and those who are not. The term that is often used around the Mediterranean is "double-speed development," or *developpement à deux vitesses.*

In societies like these, discourse on secularization, free speech and the emergence of pluralism would remain empty, ineffective and, at best, would be limited to the elite, as long as something substantial has not been done to improve the living conditions of the majority.

This is why political liberalization must go hand in hand with a developmental program that includes, first, the encouragement of entrepreneurism and the development of a middle class. Only a middle class that is educated, capable of reflection, aware of its interests and tied to a productive process will foster truly serious participation. Otherwise, we will have the usual mobilization that one-party systems have been able to develop.

One of the few historical rules of Marxism that remains viable to this day and will be so for a long time, is that there can be no democracy without a bourgeoisie. The middle class is the bulwark, the base for genuine democracy.

But one cannot limit attention to the middle class. Serious effort must be made to improve the living condition of the majority, in terms of housing, health care and education. Governments need to instill hope for the possibility of a better future, if not for this generation, at least for the next generation. This is a crucial area for competition between governments currently in power and the Islamists, because the Islamists have been very effective, it must be said, in exploiting people's misery and trying to show that they care for the people more than the existing government.

We have all followed what happened in natural disasters in Tebessa in 1989, in Algeria and Egypt in 1992, and seen how the Islamist movements were very quick to show their efficiency in bringing relief and compassion to the population, while the government reaction was ineffective and slow. In North Africa, we have great experience with the informal Islamist sector.

Among their activities are distributing books to children, distributing photocopies of textbooks for graduate students, defending squatters' rights, working hand in hand with the *trabendah* or underground markets. They have been extremely effective in developing connections with the informal economy and contraband to provide services when government has lost its welfare capacities.

The resulting situation resembles a race to get to the poor first. And unless governments are able to attend to the needs of the poor, Islamism, in its exploitative aspect, will remain with us.

When studying Islamism in historical terms, one sees that there are correlations. In Tunisia, for example, the weakening of unions has coincided with the strengthening of Islamism. In Egypt, Tunisia and Algeria, only after the weakening of the welfare state did the Islamists start presenting themselves as a counter-patronage system: "What the government cannot provide for you, we are willing to provide for you." This is a very crucial race with very large stakes.

Most of the resources used by the Islamists are state resources that are diverted to serve the Islamists' own supporters at the expense of others. But, to be fair, the Islamists are not the only patronage clientele system.

The final ingredient of this developmental

approach is the recognition that North Africa cannot face up to the Islamists and the challenge of democratization alone. North Africa cannot do it alone because the whole Mediterranean region, Europe and the United States are all involved. They need to participate in a new strategy of cooperation and aid for these countries.

This is especially important for Europe. If Europe does not want to have the side effects of Islamism and does not want to be visited by this form of protest, it really has to help these governments to liberalize economically and politically.

DOCUMENTS

SECTION A: MISCELLANEOUS

SECTION B: SELECTED STATEMENTS
BY U.S. OFFICIALS

SECTION C: SELECTED DOCUMENTS
AND STATEMENTS ON DEMOCRACY IN THE
ARAB WORLD

ALGERIA

SECTION A: MISCELLANEOUS

Freedom House Table of Independent Countries
Comparative Measures of Freedom

Country	PR	CL	Freedom Ratings
< Algeria	7<	6<	not free
Bahrain	6	5	partly free
< Egypt	5	6<	partly free
Iran	6	6<	not free
Iraq	7	7	not free
Israel	2	2	free
Jordan	3>	3>	partly free
Lebanon	5>	4	partly free
Libya	7	7	not free
Morocco	6<	5	partly free
> Oman	6	5>	partly free
Qatar	7	6<	not free
Saudi Arabia	7	7<	not free
Sudan	7	7	not free
Syria	7	7	not free
< Tunisia	6<	5	partly free
Turkey	2	4	partly free
UAE	6	5	partly free
Yemen	6	4>	partly free

Notes:
1. PR and CL stand for Political Rights and Civil Liberties. 1 represents the most free and 7 the least free category. When next to a country name, arrows facing left (<) and arrows facing right (>) indicate a general trend in freedom downward or upward respectively. When next to a number in the Political Rights or Civil Liberties columns, the arrows represent an upward or downward change caused by real world events since the last survey. The Freedom Rating is an overall judgment based on survey results.[1]

---

[1]   *Freedom Review*, January-February 1993.

Parliamentary Representation in Selected Arab Countries

COUNTRY AND ELECTION YEAR	PARTY	NUMBER OF SEATS
Algeria (1991)[1]		Total: 231
	Islamic Salvation Front (FIS)	189
	Socialist Forces Front (FFS)	25
	National Liberation Front (FLN)	15
	Independents	2
Egypt (1990)[2]		Total: 454
	National Democratic Party (NDP)	348
	Independents	83
	President's Nominees	10
	Unionist Progressive Nationalist Grouping	6

Notes:

1. Figures for the 1990 Egyptian election are incomplete. Seven members, not elected by the end of 1990 due to voting irregularities, are not included.

Jordan (1989)[3]		Total: 80
	Centrist	38
	Muslim Brotherhood	20
	Independent Islamist	13
	Leftist	9

---

[1] *Christian Science Monitor,* January 9, 1992, p. 19.
[2] *Middle East Contemporary Survey* (Boulder: Westview Press, 1990), p. 328, and Communication from U.S. Department of State, July 21, 1993.
[3] *Who is Who in Jordanian Parliament: 1989-1993* (Amman: Friedrich Ebert Stiftong, 1993).

Kuwait (1992)[1]   Total: 50

Kuwaiti Democratic Forum	2
affiliated with Kuwaiti Democratic Forum	1
endorsed by Islamic Constitutional Movement	14
Deputies Bloc	10
endorsed by Islamic Popular Grouping	9
Independents	4
Islamic Constitutional Movement	3
Islamic Patriotic Coalition	3
Islamic Popular Grouping	3
Constitutional Bloc	1

Lebanon (1992)[2]   Total: 128

Omar Karami List	21
Birri List	14
Hezbollah	12
Hoss List	9
Independents	7
Murr List	7
Syrian Social Nationalist Party (SSNP)	6
Junblatt List	5
Progressive Socialist Party (PSP)	5
Amal	4
Khatib List	4
Shuhayyib List	4
Jama'ah Islamiyyah	3
Skaff List	3
Close to Tashnag party	2
Husayni List	2
Ahmad Karami List	1
al-Wa'ad party	1
Arab Democratic party	1

---

[1] Communication from U.S. Department of State, July 23, 1993.
[2] *The Lebanon Report*, October 10, 1992, pp. 8-9.

Lebanon (cont.)

Arab Socialist Union	1
Ba'ath Arab Socialist party	1
Hentchag party	1
Hubayqah List	1
Islamic Charitable Works Association	1
Journalist	1
Popular Nasirite Organization	1
Pro-Syrian Ba'ath party	1
Solh List	1
Tashnag party	1
Union of Popular Committees	1
Union of Workers	1

Notes:

1. By the end of the secondary elections in Kesrwan-Al-Foutouh on October 11, 1992, the membership in the Lebanese parliament became complete. Five Maronites joined the parliament increasing the number of members from 123 to 128.

Yemen (1993)[1]   Total: 300

People's General Congress	122
Yemeni Congregation party	62
Yemeni Socialist party	56
Independents	48
Arabic Ba'ath party	7
Al-Haq Party	2
People's Nasserite party	1
Democratic Nasserite party	1
Al-Tashib Al-Nasir party	1

---

[1] Communication from the Embassy of Yemen, July 20, 1993.

SECTION B: SELECTED STATEMENTS
BY U.S. OFFICIALS

Edward Djerejian, Assistant Secretary of State for Near East and South Asian Affairs, Hearing of the Europe and Middle East Subcommittee of the House Foreign Affairs Committee, November 20, 1991

Question: "With respect to objectives in this region—and I'm not now just talking about the Madrid conference—is one of our objectives in the Middle East to promote democracy and pluralism?"
Djerejian: "Absolutely."

Q: "And that would apply, for example, to all the countries in the region."
Djerejian: "To all the countries."

Q: "Do we press the question of democracy and pluralism vigorously, for example, with Saudi Arabia and Kuwait?"
Djerejian: "Yes, we do. No matter what the relationship, if the countries are close friends of ours, we press the issue. If we have... a less friendly or more adversarial relationship with certain countries, we press the issue. It doesn't matter the nature of the regime. The agenda item of democratization and urging privatization is used throughout."

Q: "Let me ask you to be as specific as you can. Take the cases of Kuwait and Saudi Arabia. How do we press the issue of democracy with these governments? Who does it, at what level, and how do you press it?"
Djerejian: "Well, in the first instance, our ambassadors do it... And the president of the United States, I know, has been involved in... pressing the issue of democratization... I think democratization is one of the key issues that we deal with in our relations with the countries of the Middle East... It was even part of my mandate in Damascus to talk to the regime in Damascus about democratization and privatization."

Q: "But specifically, we have good relations with Saudi Arabia... and with Kuwait. How do we press this issue with them, and who does it?"

Djerejian: "In the first instance, it's the job of our ambassadors in their interaction with the host governments, and the issues come up in many ways. I know that our ambassador in Kuwait has raised this issue repeatedly, and we know that there are some results in terms of parliamentary elections that are scheduled in Kuwait in October of 1992, and that the Kuwaiti government is even considering seriously extending the franchise in Kuwait. So, the issue is joined in all countries, no matter what the nature of the government is. It can be a monarchy, an emirate, a republic, an authoritative regime... I think they're feeling an increasing need to demonstrate wider participation by the people in the government, and this need... is a worldwide development that really had a great deal of impetus from the events in Eastern Europe and the Soviet Union."

Q: "It's remarkable to some of us that from Central and Eastern Europe through the Soviet Union, South Africa, Central America, South America, everywhere we are dealing with [democratization and pluralism] in a very forceful fashion, but somehow the Middle East region is exempt from any pressures along these lines, which is distressing to some of us."

Djerejian: "It is not exempt. We raise [the issue] with the governments."[1]

Margaret Tutwiler, State Department Spokesman, Briefing following the cancellation of the Algerian elections and the imposition of military rule, January 13, 1992

"We view the situation [in Algeria] with concern—the interruption of the electoral process. We commend the fact that Algeria has made impressive strides toward

---

[1]   As transcribed by Federal News Service [hereinafter cited as FNS], November 20, 1991.

democracy in recent years and we hope a way can be found to resume progress as soon as possible.

"In the meantime, we urge all parties to remain calm and to find a peaceful resolution in accordance with the Algerian constitution...

"The United States has been consistent and very supportive of the moves down a democratic road in Algeria. That process appears to have been interrupted. What I am saying is that... the mechanisms that have kicked in are the ones that were set up under their constitution...

"Concerning Islamic fundamentalism, let me make three points. First, it is important not to generalize about such a complicated subject. The term 'Islamic fundamentalism' is used in different ways by different people. It embraces a wide variety of religious, political and social concepts. This is not a single coordinated international movement.

"Secondly, for many years, the United States has had productive and excellent relations with a number of Islamic or deeply observant governments and parties. We look forward to continuing doing so. The United States believes strongly in the principles of peaceful relations between neighbors, democracy and human rights. We want to continue to work with all parties to promote those principles.

"Thirdly, at the same time, we and the rest of the international community will continue to resist the efforts of extremists of whatever stripe to undermine those principles."[1]

Bill Clinton, Address to Foreign Policy Association, New York, April 1, 1992

"Promoting democracy abroad is not just a task for the American government. For years, labor unions, universities and volunteer organizations here in our nation have nurtured the democratic revolutions around the world. Without democratic institutions and values, economic

---

1   As transcribed by FNS, January 13, 1992.

reforms cannot succeed over the long run. Our nation's greatest resource is ultimately not our dollars, not our technical expertise, but our values of pluralism, enterprise, freedom and the rule of law, and the centuries of experience in making those values work for ordinary citizens. In an era of fledgling democracies, those values can be our proudest export and our most effective tool of foreign policy."[1]

Edward Djerejian, Address to the Meridian International Center, Washington, D.C., June 2, 1992

"Reviewing the main thrusts of our policy in the Middle East reminds us that, even in the 1990s, our national security interests in the region continue to exert a powerful claim on our attention. But there is more to our policy agenda than protection of vital resources and conflict resolution. Another pillar of U.S. policy is our support for human rights, pluralism, women's and minority rights, popular participation in the government and our rejection of extremism, oppression and terrorism. These worldwide issues constitute an essential part of the foundation for America's engagement with the countries of the Near East—from the Maghreb to Iran and beyond. In this context, there are certain factors which we should underscore in discussing U.S. relations with these countries.

"The first is diversity. Not only is this aiea diverse within itself, so are the relations with the countries that make it up. This diversity requires not only that a clear sense of our own values and interests guide our policy, but also that understanding and tolerance be key factors in our dealings with other political cultures.

"The second point is interaction. U.S. relations with this part of the world are just the latest chapter in a history of interaction between the West and the Middle East that is thousands of years old. Our interaction spans political, economic, social, cultural and military fields. We should not ignore this totality.

---

[1]   As transcribed by FNS, April 1, 1992.

"The third point is common aspirations. Despite obvious differences, we and the peoples of the Near East share important aspirations, which I will touch on later. These common aspirations provide a promising foundation for future cooperation.

"Politics in the region has increasingly focused on the issues of change, openness and economic and social inequities. As part of a trend that predates the events I have recounted, the role of religion has become more manifest and much attention is being paid to a phenomenon variously labeled Political Islam, the Islamic Revival or Islamic Fundamentalism.

"Uncertainty regarding this renewed Islamic emphasis abounds. Some say that it is causing a widening gap between Western values and those of the Muslim world. It is important to assess this phenomenon carefully, so that we do not fall victim to misplaced fears or faulty perceptions.

"A cover of a recent issue of the *Economist*, under the headline 'Living with Islam,' portrayed a man in traditional dress, standing in front of a mosque, and holding a gun. Inside the magazine, we are told that 'Islam resumes its march!' and that 'one anti-Westernism is growing stronger.' If there is one thought I can leave you with tonight, it is that the United States government does not view Islam as the next 'ism' confronting the West or threatening world peace. That is an overly-simplistic response to a complex reality.

"The Cold War is not being replaced with a new competition between Islam and the West. It is evident that the Crusades have been over for a long time; indeed, the ecumenical movement is the contemporary trend. Americans recognize Islam as one of the world's great faiths; it is practiced on every continent; it counts among its adherents millions of citizens of the United States. As Westerners, we acknowledge Islam as an historic civilizing force among the many that have influenced and enriched our culture. The legacy of the Muslim culture which reached the Iberian Peninsula in the Eighth Century is a rich one in the sciences, arts and culture, and in tolerance of Judaism and

Christianity. Islam acknowledges the major figures of the Judeo-Christian heritage: Abraham, Moses, and Christ.

"In countries throughout the Middle East and North Africa, we thus see groups or movements seeking to reform their societies in keeping with Islamic ideals. There is considerable diversity on how these ideals are expressed. We detect no monolithic or coordinated international effort behind these movements. What we do see are believers living in different countries placing renewed emphasis on Islamic principles, and governments accommodating Islamist political activity to varying degrees and in different ways.

"For our part as Americans, we are proud of the principles on which our country is founded. They have withstood many severe challenges over more than two centuries. We know they work. We therefore are committed to encouraging greater openness and responsiveness of political systems throughout the world.

"I am not talking here about trying to impose an American model on others. Each country must work out, in accordance with its own traditions, history and particular circumstances, how and at what pace to broaden political participation. In this respect, it is essential that there be real political dialogue between government on the one hand and other institutions on the other. Those who are prepared to take specific steps toward free elections, creating independent judiciaries, promoting the rule of law, reducing restrictions on the press, respecting the rights of minorities and guaranteeing individual rights, will find us ready to recognize and support their efforts, just as those moving in the opposite direction will find us ready to speak candidly and act accordingly. As Secretary Baker has said: We best can have truly close and enduring relations with those countries with which we share fundamental values.

"Those who seek to broaden political participation in the Middle East will, therefore, find us supportive, as we have been elsewhere in the world. At the same time, we are suspect of those who would use the democratic process to come to power, only to destroy that very process in order to retain power and political dominance. While we believe in the principle of 'one person, one vote,' we do not support 'one person, one vote, one time.'

"Let me make it very clear with whom we differ: We differ with those, regardless of religion, who practice terrorism, oppress minorities, preach intolerance or violate internationally accepted standards of conduct regarding human rights; with those who are insensitive to the need for political pluralism; with those who cloak their message in another brand of authoritarianism; with those who substitute religious and political confrontation for constructive engagement with the rest of the world; with those who do not share our commitment to peaceful resolution of conflict, especially the Arab-Israeli conflict; and with those who would pursue their goals through repression and violence.

"It is for just these reasons that we have such basic differences with the avowedly secular governments in Iraq and Libya. To the extent that other governments pursue or adopt similar practices, we will distance ourselves from them, regardless of whether they describe their approach in secular, religious or any other terms. Simply-stated, religion is not a detriment—positive or negative—in the nature or quality of our relations with other countries. Our quarrel is with extremism, and the violence, denial, intolerance, intimidation, coercion and terror which too often accompany it.

"The facts bear that out. The United States has good, productive relations with countries and peoples of all religions throughout the world, including many whose systems of government are firmly grounded in Islamic principles. Religious freedom and tolerance are integral elements of our American national character and constitutional system. Indeed, as much as any society, the American people understand the meaning of diversity and the virtues of tolerance.

"The broad policy goals of the United States in the Near East region have been laid out by President Bush and Secretary Baker: genuine peace between Israel and its Arab neighbors; enhancing security and deterring or defeating aggression; helping to protect the world's economic security;

promoting economic and social justice; and promoting the values in which we believe.

"I believe these are the aspirations in which the peoples of the region—whether Muslim, Jewish, Christian or otherwise—can realistically share. Like us, they seek a peaceful, better future. They aspire to work productively in peace and safety to feed, house and clothe their families; in which they can have a say and can find personal fulfillment and justice. In this respect, the pursuit of viable economic and social development programs, privatization and adequate educational and vocational training opportunities, are key to responding to the basic material needs of the region's people.

"Working with an international community of unprecedented solidarity, we have come a long way in the past few years in repelling aggression and in promoting a negotiated peace to a seemingly intractable conflict in the region. We still have a long way to go before these worthy efforts will have achieved success and before other aspirations we share are realized. We can get there through close engagement and constructive interaction between the United States and all the countries of the Near East region at all levels: government-to-government, group-to-group, person-to-person and faith-to-faith."[1]

Bill Clinton, Address to Los Angeles World Affairs Council, August 13, 1992

"My administration will stand up for democracy. We will offer international assistance to emerging fragile democracies...

"We will stand by Israel, our only democratic ally in the Middle East, and, while supporting the peace process, will press for more accountable governance throughout the region, work for demilitarization and make sure that weapons of mass destruction do not enter the hands of

---

1 *Mideast Mirror*, June 4, 1992.

tyrants all too willing to use them."[1]

Bill Clinton, excerpt from Putting People First, September 1992

Israel and the Middle East

"The end of the Cold War does not mean the end of U.S. responsibility abroad, especially in the Middle East. The people of the region are still denied peace and democracy. America's friend, Israel, is still threatened by her neighbors.

"The United States has vital interests in the Middle East. That is why we supported President Bush's efforts to throw Saddam Hussein out of Kuwait. We must remain engaged in the region and continue to promote the spread of democracy, human rights and free markets.

"Among all the countries in the Middle East, only Israel has experienced the peaceful transfer of power by ballot— not by bullet. We will never let Israel down..."

Democracy

"Our foreign policy must promote democracy as well as stability. We cannot, as the Bush-Quayle administration has done, ignore the link between the two.

"We should promote democracy in the Middle East and throughout the world. The Bush-Quayle administration lost an opportunity to promote democracy in Kuwait.

"A Clinton-Gore administration will never forge strategic relationships with dangerous, despotic regimes. Bush failed to learn from his appeasement of Saddam Hussein when he shared intelligence with him, awarded him credits and opposed sanctions until the invasion of Kuwait. Today the Bush administration repeats the same mistake as it casts a blind eye on Syria's human rights abuses and on its support for terrorism."[2]

---

1   As transcribed by FNS, August 13, 1992.
2   Bill Clinton, *Putting People First* (New York: Times Books, 1992).

Edward Djerejian, Address to the National Association of Arab Americans, September 11, 1992

"U.S. policy toward Lebanon remains firm and consistent. This policy was reiterated to both the Syrian and Lebanese leadership... We support full implementation of both the letter and the spirit of the Ta'if Accord and the withdrawal of all non-Lebanese forces from Lebanon, and we have repeatedly made this clear to all concerned parties. The Ta'if Accord requires coordination now by the governments of Lebanon and Syria on the decision to redeploy Syrian troops to the western entrances to the Bekaa Valley. In our view, that decision should be taken by both governments this month with redeployment occurring shortly thereafter and as soon as possible. It also requires the completion of the process of disarming all militias, particularly Hezbollah. Implementation of this agreement helped bring to an end the turbulent era of civil war in Lebanon. With full adherence and compliance of the parties of the Ta'if agreement, we believe it will offer the best chance of restoring the unity, independence, sovereignty and territorial integrity of Lebanon.

"Lebanon recently conducted three rounds of voting to elect a new parliament. These were the first parliamentary elections held in Lebanon since 1972 and the tragic civil war which so ravaged Lebanon and its people. In the weeks leading to the election, we repeatedly called for free and fair voting held in an environment devoid of intimidation and coercion. We consistently stated that the decision to proceed with elections at this time was that of the Lebanese government to make. Similarly, the decision of some Lebanese political figures not to participate was theirs to make.

"The United States is clearly disappointed that the elections were not prepared and conducted in a manner to ensure the broadest national consensus. The turnout of eligible voters in some locations was extremely low. There were also widespread reports of irregularities, which might have been avoided had there been impartial international observers at hand. As a consequence, the results do not reflect the full spectrum of the Lebanese body politic.

"We fervently hope that the Lebanese people and their government will renew their commitment to national reconciliation and to the unity and sovereignty they deserve. We will continue to support the expansion of the authority of the central institutions of the Lebanese government and the Lebanese armed forces throughout Lebanon, and we will continue to work with other countries and international organizations to encourage and support the Lebanese people as they get on with the priority task of reconstruction...

"Finally, I would like to say a few words about our efforts to promote the values we Americans cherish and which form the foundation of all that has made this country great. These fundamental values, which underlie U.S. foreign policy globally—basic human rights, popular participation in government, pluralism and minority and women's rights—also find reflection in our approach to the countries of the Near East, including the Arab states of North Africa...

"We are wary of those who would use the democratic process to come to power, only to destroy that very process in order to retain political dominance."[1]

Bill Clinton, Address on "Democracy In America," Milwaukee, October 1, 1992

"Let there be no mistake, this world is still a dangerous place. Military power still matters. And I am committed to maintaining a strong and ready defense. I will use that strength where necessary to defend our vital interests. But power must be accompanied by clear purpose.

"Mr. Bush's ambivalence about supporting democracy, his eagerness to befriend potentates and dictators has shown itself time and again. It has been a disservice not only to our democratic values, but also to our national

---

1   *U.S. Department of State Dispatch*, September 14, 1992.

interests. For in the long run, I believe Mr. Bush's neglect of our democratic ideals abroad could do as much harm as his neglect of our economic needs at home.

"The administration has sometimes treated the conflict between Israel and the Arab states as just another quarrel between religions and nations rather than one in which the survival of a democratic ally—Israel—has been at stake. I support strongly the peace talks that are under way, and if elected, I will continue without interruption America's role in them.

"I also believe that American policy in the Middle East should be guided by a vision of the region in which our Israeli and Arab partners are secure in their peace and where the practices and principles of both personal liberty and governmental accountability are spreading. For example, I believe we can and must work with others to help build a more democratic and more free Lebanon. This pattern continues in other parts of the world.

"It is the powerful appeal of our democratic values and our enduring political institutions to people around the world that make us special. That does not mean we can embark on reckless crusades that we can force every ideal, including the promotion of democracy on other people. Our actions must be tempered with prudence and common sense. We know that ballot boxes alone do not solve every world problem and that some countries and cultures are many steps away from democratic institutions. We know there may be times when other security needs or economic interests even in the aftermath of the bipolar Cold War world will diverge from our commitment to democracy and human rights. We know we cannot support every group's hopes for self-determination. We know that the dissolution of old and repressive empires will often be complex and contentious.

"Moreover, we know there will always be those in the world who pursue their goals through force and violence. But they should know that a Clinton administration will maintain the military strength we need to defend our people, our vital interests and our values."[1]

Marlin Fitzwater, White House Press Secretary, Statement on free elections in Kuwait, October 7, 1992

"The president is pleased to note that this week Kuwait held free parliamentary elections. The United States has been a strong supporter of this process since the amir's decision to hold elections was announced during the Iraqi occupation. We have also been encouraged by the statement by the crown prince that the Kuwaiti government will soon propose legislation to amend the constitution to broaden the electorate and specifically to give women the right to vote in future elections. The amir and the Kuwaiti people are to be congratulated on this latest stage in Kuwait's progress toward full recovery and reconstruction.

"These elections reaffirm Kuwait's hard-won independence and the freedoms enjoyed by the Kuwaiti people, in sharp contrast to the agony the Iraqi people still endure from Saddam. The gulf between Kuwait's determination to begin a democratic process and Saddam's brutalities against the Iraqi people is a vivid reminder of why the coalition had no choice but to use force to liberate Kuwait. The United States remains committed both to supporting Kuwait in its physical and political reconstruction and to support the efforts of the Iraqi opposition toward building a democratic future for the people of Iraq."[2]

Warren Christopher, Senate Confirmation Hearing, January 13, 1993

"Not since the late 1940s has our nation faced the challenge of shaking and shaping an entirely new foreign policy for a world that is fundamentally changed. Like our counterparts, we need to design a new strategy for protecting

---

1   As transcribed by FNS, October 1, 1992.
2   *Presidential Documents*, October 12, 1992.

American interests around the world by laying the foundations for a more just and more stable world. That strategy must take into account and reflect fundamental changes that have been made in the world in recent times. These include the surfacing of long-suppressed ethnic, religious and sectional conflicts (especially in the former Soviet bloc), the globalization of commerce and capital, a world-wide democratic revolution fueled by new information technologies that amplify the power of ideas, new and old human rights challenges (including protecting ethnic minorities as well as political dissidents), the rise of new security threats especially terrorism and the spread of advanced weaponry and weapons of mass destruction...

"To adapt our foreign policy and institution to these changes, President-elect Clinton has stressed that our effort must rest on three pillars. First, we must elevate America's economic security as a primary goal of foreign policy. Second, we must preserve our military strength as we adapt our forces to new security challenges. And third, we must organize our foreign policy around the goal of promoting the spread of democracy and free markets abroad...

"Our new diplomacy will encourage the global revolution for democracy that is transforming the world. Promoting democracy, of course, does not imply a crusade to make the world exactly in our image, rather, support for democracy and human rights abroad can and should be a central tenet of our own efforts to improve our security. Democratic movements are not only more likely to protect human and minority rights, they are also much more likely to resolve ethnic, religious and territorial disputes in a peaceful manner. And they are much more likely to be reliable partners in diplomacy, trade, arms accords and global environmental protection.

"A strategic approach to promoting democracy requires that we coordinate all of our leverage; such elements as trade, economic and security assistance and debt relief [must all be used] in the promotion of democracy. By enlisting international and regional institutions in the work of promoting democracy, the U.S. can leverage its own limited resources and avoid the appearance of trying to dominate others...

"Democracy cannot be imposed from the top down, but must be built from the bottom up. Our policy should be to encourage patient, sustained efforts to help build the institutions that make democracy possible: political parties, free media, laws that protect property and individual rights, an impartial judiciary, labor unions and voluntary associations that stand between the individual and the state...

"The three pillars of our foreign policy—economic growth, military strength and support for democracy—are mutually reinforcing. A vibrant economy will strengthen America's hand abroad while permitting us to maintain a strong military without sacrificing domestic needs. By helping others forge democracy out of the ruins of dictatorship, we can pacify old threats, prevent new ones and create new markets for U.S. trade and investment...

"In the Middle East... we must maintain the momentum behind the current negotiations over peace and regional issues. President Bush and Secretary Baker deserve great credit for bringing the Arabs and the Israelis to the bargaining table, and the Clinton administration is committed to carrying on these negotiations, taking advantage of this historic breakthrough.

"Our democracy-centered policy underscores our special relationship with Israel, the region's only democracy, with whom we are committed to maintain a strong and vibrant strategic relationship. We also believe that America's unswerving commitment to Israel and Israel's right to exist behind secure borders is essential to a just and lasting peace. We will continue our efforts with both Israel and our Arab friends to address the full range of the region's challenge.

"Throughout the Middle East and the Persian Gulf, we will work toward new arms control agreements, particularly concerning weapons of mass destruction. We will assume a vigilant stance toward both Iran and Iraq and even beyond. In this region as well, we will champion economic reform, more accountable governance and increased respect for human rights. Following a decade in which over a thousand Americans were killed, injured or kidnapped by perpetrators of international terrorism, we will give no quarter to terrorists or the states that sponsor their crimes against humanity."[1]

Warren Christopher, Address to the Arab-American Anti-Discrimination Council Conference, Arlington, Virginia, April 23, 1993

"The promotion of democracy and respect for human rights is one of the three pillars of President Clinton's foreign policy. I know, however, that there is a concern both within and outside the region over Islamic fundamentalism and its effect on the stability and policies of many of these countries.

"Tonight, I would like to clearly tell you that Islam is not our enemy. We do not consider Islam a threat to world peace or regional security. What we do oppose is extremism or fanaticism whether of religious or secular nature.

"We part company with those who preach intolerance, abuse human rights, or resort to violence in pursuit of political goals. While we certainly cannot impose our own form of government on others, we strongly support those who share and seek to encourage democratic values in their countries. As with the peace process, the United States stands ready to work with our friends in the region toward the important goals of peace, stability and social justice.

"In the end, of course, it will be up to the people of the region and the governments of the Middle East to shape their own future. If they are successful, the benefits of true peace and prosperity will fall to future generations of Muslims, Jews and Christians. It will be the first time that it has done so in these ancient lands.

"I want you to know that the president and this secretary of state intend to move the peace process forward. We intend to remain engaged and we hope to earn and retain the trust of all parties to this historic quest for

---

[1]   As transcribed by FNS, January 13, 1993.

peace."[1]

Richard Boucher, State Department Spokesman, Statement on Secretary Christopher's meeting with Iraqi opposition leaders, April 27, 1993

"Secretary Christopher met today with a delegation led by the Presidential Council of the Iraqi National Congress.

"The secretary emphasized the importance of Iraq complying fully with all UN Security Council resolutions, including those on ceasing repression of the Iraqi people. He added that he found it inconceivable that Saddam Hussein could obey those resolutions and stay in power but hoped that pressing the resolutions can ensure his departure from power. The secretary stressed U.S. commitment to seeing a future democratic, pluralistic government in Iraq which can live in peace with its own people and respect its neighbors. He acknowledged the success of the INC in uniting the diverse religious and ethnic groups that make up Iraq.

"Highlighting the U.S. concern over the human rights situation in Iraq, the secretary told them that the United States will propose that the Security Council consider the creation of a commission to investigate Iraqi war crimes, crimes against humanity and genocide. He added that the United States also supported UN Special Rapporteur Max van der Stoel's call for the assigning of UN human rights monitors throughout Iraq...

"The secretary concluded by noting that only through democracy, respect for human rights, equal treatment of Iraq's people and adherence to basic norms of international behavior could Iraq be brought back into the community of civilized nations. The INC will have the support of the United States in achieving these goals."[2]

---

1   As transcribed by FNS, April 23, 1993.

2   *U.S. Department of State Dispatch,* May 3, 1993.

State Department Spokesman, U.S. Department of State, Statement on Yemeni elections, April 28, 1993

"The United States congratulates the people and government of Yemen on the success of their first multiparty elections.

"On April 27, Yemen held free, multiparty, parliamentary elections, open to all adult citizens. These successful elections were the culmination of a commendable decision, made by the Yemenis themselves at the time of the unification of the two independent Yemeni states in May 1990, to create a multiparty democracy in their new country.

"International election specialists, including representatives of non-governmental organizations from the United States and other nations, were invited in by Yemeni officials both to observe the elections and to offer technical advice in developing electoral procedures. Yemenis at all levels, public and private, took it upon themselves to create an electoral framework within which Yemen could begin its movement to democracy. We also note positively Yemen's declared commitment to human rights and a market economy.

"The United States looks forward to working with the government to be formed as a result of these elections."[1]

Edward Djerejian, Testimony before House Foreign Affairs Committee, May 12, 1993

"Like so much of the developing world these days, the Maghreb is a region being buffeted by the winds of change. There is a growing popular participation, for economic opportunity and social justice. The countries of the Maghreb are responding in different ways to these trends, which in some cases involve political, economic, social and even violent challenges to the governments involved.

"Secretary Christopher has made clear that the

---

1   *U.S. Department of State Dispatch*, May 3, 1993.

promotion of democracy and respect for human rights form one of the major pillars of the Clinton administration's foreign policy. Our policy towards the countries of the Maghreb reflect that reality.

"It also reflects the reality that Maghreb today is on the cutting edge of a phenomenon affecting much of the Middle East, a phenomenon known as political Islam... Experience suggests to us that political Islamic movements are to an important degree rooted in worsening socioeconomic conditions in individual countries. While political Islam takes many forms, and varies considerably from one country to another, our approach to the phenomenon can be outlined in a few basic points... First, Islam, one of the world's great religions, is not our enemy.

"Second, what we do oppose is extremism and fanaticism, whether of religious or secular nature. We part company with those who preach intolerance, abuse human rights or resort to violence in pursuit of their goals.

"And, third, while we cannot impose our own form of government on others, or wish to do so, we strongly support those who share and seek to encourage democratic values in their own countries... The United States stands ready to work with our friends in the region toward the important goals of peace, stability and social justice..."[1]

---

1   As transcribed by FNS, May 12, 1993.

SECTION C: SELECTED DOCUMENTS AND STATEMENTS ON DEMOCRACY IN THE MIDDLE EAST

ALGERIA

Sheikh Abdelkader Hachani, acting leader of the Islamic Salvation Front (FIS), Interview, November 20, 1991

Question: "What will happen if the elections are held and if the FIS remains outside the political institutions, i.e., outside the next parliament?"

Hachani: "As far as we [are] concerned, our presence in various state institutions is not a goal. It is a means to realize other objectives. We want the religion of Almighty God to prevail and to mobilize all the nation for the cause of God so that God's will may be everything. As far as we are concerned, our political exercise is not... [changes thought] It would be interesting for us to be present in these institutions, and participating in the elections would be a fundamental thing, but if we do not participate in the elections we will continue our political activity, with the will of Almighty God. Everything is with the permission of God, and God knows better."[1]

Prime Minister Sid Ahmed Ghozali, News conference, January 6, 1992

"Immediately after my appointment as head of this government, I made the following statement: I pledge to you that I will do my utmost to provide the necessary assurances for organizing free and clean elections.

"This is what the government has done... But when we talk about the freedom of the elections and their cleanness, this freedom and this cleanness could not be achieved by one side only; in other words, one needs two hands to clap. In order to achieve this freedom and this cleanness, all the

---

1   Radio Algiers Network, November 20, 1991, as printed in *Foreign Broadcast Information Service* [hereinafter cited as FBIS], November 21.

parties must work for that purpose...

"Unfortunately, [I cannot] say in my capacity as prime minister, that the elections in the first round were characterized by the required level of freedom and cleanness which we sought in erneast to achieve...

"These elections have brought to us all a strong, clear and loud message, one that comes equally from the citizens who voted and those who did not participate. The message is that the citizens are feeling great frustration, indeed desperation. This message is, on the one hand, one of complete rejection, and on the other hand, a demand for radical change...

"We now face a painful paradox for this government, which came with a pledge, committed and promised to prepare free and clean legislative elections in order to entrench democracy in this homeland. Now this government, along with the majority of its citizens, fears that this process could become merely a tool to eliminate democracy. Moreover, the Algerian government—and I emphasize it—the majority of Algerian men and women now fear for Algeria's fate itself. Thus, the Algerian people are once again at a crossroads. The dangers are serious, real and numerous. However, I am convinced that the Algerian people have sufficient material and human potential and moral capabilities to allow them to overcome the ordeals, and to confront the challenges with brilliant success."[1]

President Chadli Bendjedid, Letter of resignation, January 11, 1992

"Brothers, sisters, citizens: No doubt you know that I was not desirous of being elected to the post of president of the republic in the aftermath of the death of the late President Houari Boumedienne. My acceptance of the election was only to comply with the wish and persistence of my comrades. Even at the time I knew that it was both a

---

[1] ENTV Television Network, January 5, 1993, as printed in *FBIS*, January 6.

heavy responsibility and a great honor. Since then, I have been trying to perform my tasks with the utmost conscientiousness and a sense of duty. My conviction has been that the Algerian people should be given the means to fully express their will, especially because they already once before paid a high price for regaining their position on the international scene. Therefore, as soon as conditions permitted, I worked to open the democratic course necessary for the completion of the achievements of the liberation revolution.

"Here we are today living a democratic and pluralistic experiment, one characterized by many excesses, in the midst of an environment marked by extremely conflicting currents. Therefore, the measures taken and the systems demanded to resolve our problems have today reached a point which cannot be overstepped without grave and imminent harm to national coherence and to the preservation of public order and national unity.

"No doubt signs of this situation are no longer a secret. In the face of the extent of this unexpected danger, I consider in the depth of my heart and consciousness that the initiatives being taken are not likely to guarantee peace and harmony among the citizens at this time.

"In the face of these grave developments, I have thought at great length about the critical situation and possible solutions. The sole result that I arrived at is that I cannot continue performing my duties without harming the sacred pledge I made to the nation.

"Being aware of the responsibilities at this historic moment that our nation has reached, I consider that the only solution to the current crisis lies in my withdrawal from the political scene. For that reason, brothers, sisters and citizens, as of today I relinquish the duties of president of the republic.

"I ask each and every one of you to consider this decision a sacrifice on my part in the nation's best interests."[1]

---

[1]   As read on ENTV Television Network, January 11, 1993, and printed in *FBIS*, January 13.

State Higher Security Council, Statement, January 12, 1992

"... Noting the state of a constitutional vacuum resulting from the coincidence of the vacancy in the presidency with the resignation and the People's National Assembly through dissolution... the Higher Security Council has decided unanimously:

"First, it is noted that it is impossible to continue the election process until the necessary conditions for the normal functioning of institutions, as stipulated by the Constitutional Council, are fulfilled.

"Second, it decided temporarily to take over every matter liable to infringe on public order and the security of the state.

"Third, it announces that it is in an open session and is meeting without interruption to fulfill its obligations until a solution is found by the institutional bodies who are notified of the vacancy in the presidency."[1]

Higher Security Council Blueprint for Transition to Democracy, June 21, 1993

• The Higher Security Council will step down by the end of this year at the latest and be replaced by a president and two vice presidents.

• Since presidential and legislative elections are not possible now for known "technical and political reasons," a transitional period of at least two years and a maximum of three years is needed to ease the country into a democratic system that would restore the electoral process and consolidate the republic's institutions. During this period, the Constitution of 1989, with the exception of the provisions relating to the presidency and the legislative authority, will remain in force.

• During the transitional period, the constitution will be reviewed and amended, with special attention paid to the articles dealing with political parties and the media.

---

[1]   ENTV Television Network, January 12, 1992, as printed in *FBIS*, January 13.

The authority of the state will be restored, the election lists will be reviewed, the local and central administrations will be reorganized and the legislative authority will be strengthened.

• The ultimate target of the transitional period is to eliminate the "three types of monopoly that characterized past practices:

"1. Political monopoly must give way to the principle of the alternation of power by democratic elections.

"2. The ideological monopoly must be replaced by political pluralism, freedom of expression and thought.

"3. The state's monopoly on the economy must give way to a market economy, the economy of [private] initiative, although the state will remain present as the driving force of national economic life and also as operator in certain strategic sectors." A change in the economic system is necessary, although it is bound to be socially painful.

• For the purposes of the transitional period, the advisory council will be reconstituted, bringing into it representatives of government agencies, political parties and associations and giving it legislative powers. "Higher councils" will also be formed to study the principal questions of Islam, socioeconomic affairs, youth and education affairs.

• Islam will remain the state religion and "one of the basic elements of society," but action must be undertaken to correct some of the misconceptions that have been associated with it.

• Arabic will be the official language of the Algerian nation, but the heritage of all sectors of the population will be taken into consideration, with special reference to the Berbers.[1]

---

[1]   As reported in *al-Sharq al-Awsat* and Reuters and printed in *Mideast Mirror*, June 23, 1993.

EGYPT

President Hosni Mubarak, News conference, December 16, 1992

Question: "One of the objectives of terrorism is obviously to strike at the stability and great democracy we are experiencing. At the same time, confronting terrorism could harm democracy. This is usually a very difficult equation or process. To what extent can we balance confronting terrorism and preserving democracy?"

Mubarak: "We will not divert from democracy. Therefore, we will confront terrorism through legitimacy and the law. Other countries might cancel the law and constitution and take very violent measures. I am not an advocate of such moves. I do not want the people of Egypt to enter a new phase of totalitarianism or violence. The objective of all this terrorism is to force an undemocratic regime on the country. Those who like this type of talk... do not want democracy, even though they might pretend to be democratic. These are totalitarian regimes. Under no circumstances will we allow them to take over. We should not fear this or fear dealing with terrorism legitimately.

"We will not divert from democracy. Democracy is very harsh on those who divert from it... I am careful to keep all our measures [of confronting terrorism] within the limits of legitimacy, so that we can all learn that the right road runs through legitimate channels. Our democracy will collapse if we resort to illegitimate methods.

"Does democracy mean letting things get out of hand even when I have authorities to rectify things that hurt the country? If we had done that, things would have taken the same course they have taken in other countries; we would have lost our legitimacy. What could we do then? The country would have regressed. If tourism is declining now, it could have stopped completely. Investors would have panicked and transferred their money abroad. Who would have been hurt? The Egyptian citizen; he would have failed to manage or to find a job. Unemployment would have increased. The world is trying to increase production and open factories to create jobs for citizens. If we do not use our authority within a democratic and legitimate framework, it could lead to a serious setback that would affect the Egyptian citizen primarily. I am anxious to protect the Egyptian citizen with all means at my disposal. I make every possible effort to promote democracy, which takes care of the citizen. If I have a certain authority and fail to use it, what will happen?...

"If these authorities are abused, be sure that no one in the parties or the parliament would keep silent. We use the authority at the proper time and place. Our goal is to safeguard the Egyptian citizen's life and livelihood."[1]

Sheikh Omar Abdel Rahman, Interview in Uktubar, December 20, 1992

Question: "What are your demands?"
Rahman: "Our main demands are to let God's *sharia* be the law, to rule according to God's book, to release the detainees, and to free those who speak the truth from oppression."

Q: "What is your relationship with the Islamic groups in Egypt?"
Rahman: "My relationship with them is that of a defender of the truth... I address my words to the government, because my objective is that the Egyptian government rule by the word of God."

Q: "How do see you the application of the *sharia* in Egypt?"
Rahman: "The regime must be removed and *ulema* should take over and implement God's *sharia*."

Q: "How do you feel about democracy under an Islamic government?"
Rahman: "Islam calls for *shura* [rule by consultation],

---

[1] ESC Television, January 16, 1992, as printed in *FBIS*, December 17, 1992.

which is better than democracy. If democracy clearly implies *shura*, then Islam approves it. If democracy means freedom of movement and meeting, the existence of groups, such as parties that express what they want and elections, we, of course, have reservations. By the way, democracy has not yet been implemented in Egypt."

Q: "You said before that Islam rejects democracy because it means the rule of the people by the people, and in Islam the rule is by God alone. How can we imagine a *shura* system in the computer age? How can we apply such a system in a country with a population of 56 million people?"

Rahman: "If democracy means freedom of opinion for all, we accept this. But the rule in an Islamic system is the rule of God alone, according to *sharia*, the Koran, and the Prophet's teachings. No one has the right to make a ruling except on the basis of what came from God."[1]

President Hosni Mubarak, Interview in Der Spiegel, January 25, 1993

"Former Algerian President Chadli Bendjedid told me at one time that he would give all parties, including the religious parties, complete leeway because this would strengthen his government. It did not work."

Question: "Repression does not stop religious militancy. Wouldn't democracy be a better deterrent?"

Mubarak: "Yes, democracy and openness are our sharpest weapons. We always tell our people the whole truth.

Q: "Do the Islamic extremists also enjoy freedom of expression?"

Mubarak: "The Islamic politicians only want power. Once they are in power, the democratic liberties are forgotten. If we tolerated an Islamic party, a Christian party would be founded soon after. Religion would be misused, and Muslims

---

1   *Uktubar*, December 22, 1992, as printed in *FBIS*, December 22, 1992.

and Christians would fight each other. That is why we do not permit religious parties in Egypt."

Q: "Could an Algerian situation develop on the Nile?"
Mubarak: "I do not think that would be possible. If the Algerians had kept to their constitution, which prohibits the forming of religious parties, developments would have been different."[1]

President Hosni Mubarak, Interview in al-Anba, March 17, 1993

Question: "Do you attribute the Islamic upsurge in Egypt to economic conditions?"
Mubarak: "First we must be specific about the concept so that we will not be confused. If the talk is about Islamic upsurge, Egypt has been an Islamic state throughout its history and its people are Muslim. Egypt is the country where al-Azhar, the beacon of Islam, is located. Within al-Azhar, preachers and *ulema* live and move about with their genuine thought. They represent the most predominant and overwhelming trend for Muslims and Islam through moderation.

"As for the extremist upsurge meant by your question, it is not a proper Islamic upsurge. This extremist upsurge is just a tool used by some forces, whether abroad or within, that seek through this trend to impose hegemony and guardianship in the name of Islam.

"The confrontation in Egypt is between a moderate Islam and intellectual extremism hiding behind the name of Islam. This extremism will not survive in Egypt because the people are wary, comprehending and know the facts. That a few terrorists could control all [of] our society is inconceivable. Thus, we are talking about terrorism, terrorists and outlaws. This breed of people is present [even] in rich countries..."

---

1   *Der Spiegel*, January 25, 1993, as printed in *FBIS*, January 28.

Q: "Do you believe that the Islamic upsurge has been able to project itself in this manner because of a political vacuum?"

Mubarak: "Let us discuss the matter with a degree of logic and tolerance. You hear of an Islamic upsurge in Egypt because we are a democratic country that guarantees free press and the right of expression and [we] live in a truly democratic atmosphere. On the contrary, had the regime in Egypt been dictatorial, no one would have heard of an Islamic upsurge.

"You do not hear about it in some countries although an Islamic upsurge exists in them. These countries deal with such currents with force and summary annihilation... Here in Egypt both the state and the people are against trading in Islam and terrifying peaceful citizens in the name of Islam."[1]

Sheikh Omar Abdel Rahman, Interview in al-Hayat, March 18, 1993

"Democracy was not an option for the Islamists. 'The experiment has failed in Jordan, in Egypt and also in Algeria, where it failed miserably.'

"[Rahman] said what happened in Algeria 'proves our point—that the rulers will not allow Islam to work freely... Although we differed with our brothers in the FIS over the utility of democracy and elections, we used to always pray for their success.

"'We used to say that what is taken by democracy can be [lost] by democracy. Islam's coming to power will not be through democracy.'"[2]

Sheikh Omar Abdel Rahman, Interview in the New Yorker, April 12, 1993

Question: "Are Jama'at [the Islamic group] and al-Jihad

---

1   *Al-Jumhuriyah,* March 13, 1993, as printed in *FBIS,* March 17.
2   *Mideast Mirror,* March 18, 1993.

religious movements or political movements?"

Rahman: "In Christianity, you have a separation of church and state. Because the church resisted the modernization of Europe, it was pushed aside. But Islam is very different: it covers every aspect of life—politics and economics, religion and social issues, science and knowledge. Therefore, it is not possible to differentiate between religion and politics. In Islam, you cannot be a Muslim unless you know politics. We do not follow the axiom 'Leave what is for Caesar for Caesar and what is for God for God.'"

Q: "At your trial in the Sadat assassination case, you told the judge that it was lawful to shed the blood of a ruler who does not rule according to God's ordinances—"

Rahman: "Yes. I testified for twelve hours before the judge, and I told him that whoever does not rule as God orders is an infidel. And if you apply that rule to Nasser, Sadat and Mubarak, they are all infidels...

"It was Sadat himself who issued the *fatwa* to be killed, by moving away from his religion and imprisoning his people. And it was his own people who killed him, and this will be Mubarak's fate as well..."

Q: "What kind of Islamic state do you want in Egypt? What is the role model? Iran? Saudi Arabia? Sudan?"

Rahman: "It will be closer to the example of Sudan. Saudi Arabia does not apply Islamic rules... They give their people absolutely no freedoms. Their jails are full—full of innocent people. This is not Islam. Their Islam is cosmetic, with only one purpose in mind: to keep the ruling family on the throne. What we want is a true Islamic state. We want a state where there will be no poverty, where freedom is guaranteed. We will rule through a *shura*, or consultative council, which in the West you call democracy."

Q: "What would the imposition of *sharia* mean for Egypt's non-Muslims?"

Rahman: "Islam guarantees the rights of Jews and Christians under Islamic law: let them practice their religion and protect their houses of worship. There will be no pressure to convert. But in the meantime it is very well known that no minority in any country has its own laws.'[1]

IRAQ

Charter 91, a bill of rights for a free Iraq originally drafted by Kanan Makiya, has been signed by Iraqis of all persuasions, Sunni, Shi'ite and Kurdish. Its name is a reference to Charter 77, a Czech paper demanding human rights in Eastern Europe.

Civil society in Iraq has been continuously violated by state in the name of ideology. As a consequence the networks through which civility is normally produced and reproduced have been destroyed. A collapse of values in Iraq has therefore coincided with the destruction of the public realm for uncoerced human association. In these conditions, the first task of a new politics is to reject barbarism and reconstitute civility.

With this is mind, we the undersigned, a group of men and women from Iraq comprised of different nationalities, religious denominations, ideological and political convictions, hereby declare:

1. People have rights for no other reason than that they exist as individual human beings.

2. Freedom from fear is the essential prerequisite for realizing the inherent dignity of the human person.
Specifically, freedom from fear requires that a new Iraqi constitution provide that:
• The quality of being an Iraqi shall never again be held in doubt because of faith, belief or presumed loyalty.
• Citizenship become the irrevocable right of every individual born in Iraq, or to an Iraqi parent or naturalized by an Iraqi state.
• No Iraqi be subjected to arbitrary arrest or detention or

---

[1] Mary Anne Weaver, "The Trail of the Sheikh," *The New Yorker*, April 12, 1993.

deportation.
• No Iraqi be subjected to cruel, inhuman or degrading treatment or punishment.
• No confession of guilt, however obtained, be considered admissible in an Iraqi court of law.
• A moratorium on capital punishment be promulgated for a period of not less than ten years.
• Liability for punishment be always individual, never collective.
• Unrestricted freedom of travel within and outside the boundaries of Iraq be an absolute and inalienable right of every citizen.
• The villages, towns, cities, water sources, forests and historic and religious sites of Iraq be declared a national trust which no political authority can capriciously destroy, disfigure or relocate.
• The Universal Declaration of Human Rights, adopted and proclaimed by the United Nations General Assembly resolution 217 A (III) of 10 December 1948, be considered binding and constitutive of the legal system of Iraq.
• Any Iraqi official found to have violated the above be dismissed and prosecuted to the fullest extent of the law.

3. Rebuilding civil society means elevating the principle of toleration into a new public norm soaring above all ideologies.

Toleration in matters of politics, religion and ethnic feeling is the only true alternative to violence and the rule of fear. The full creative potential of Iraqis, in which we deeply believe, will only be realized when toleration burns as fiercely in individual hearts and minds as it does in the new constitution of Iraq...

4. Representative parliamentary democracy is the rule in the Republic of Tolerance.

Democracy requires coordinating the representation of differences among people on three levels: within civil society; between civil society and the state; and between the executive, legislative and judicial realms of government. Democracy is not only ruling in the name of the people, nor is it simply majority rule. Central to democracy is the constitutionally guaranteed set of rights which protect the part from tyranny of the whole. The fundamental idea is that the majority rules only because it is a majority, not because it has a monopoly on the truth...

5. The notion that strength resides in large standing armies and up-to-date weapons of destruction has proved bankrupt.

Real strength is always internal—in the creative, cultural and wealth-producing capabilities of a people. It is found in civil society, not in the army or in the state. Armies often threaten democracy; the larger they grow the more they weaken civil society. This is what happened in Iraq. Therefore, conditional upon international and regional guarantees which secure the territorial integrity of Iraq, preferably within the framework of an overall reduction in the levels of militarization of the whole Middle East, a new Iraqi constitution should:

• Abolish conscription and reorganize the army into a professional, small and purely defensive force which will never be used for internal repression.

• Set an absolute upper limit on expenditure on this new force equal to 2 percent of Iraqi national income.

• Have as its first article the following: "aspiring sincerely to an international peace based on justice and order, the Iraqi people forever renounce war as a sovereign right of the nation and the threat or use of force as a means of settling international disputes. The right of belligerency of the Iraqi state will not be recognized."[1]

Jalal Talabani, General Secretary of the Patriotic Union of Kurdistan (PUK), Address to Council on Foreign Relations, September 27, 1991

"Dictatorship, therefore, is truly a threat to Iraq's national unity and integrity. It is a source of inter-ethnic

---

1   See Amity Shlaes, "The Voice of Iraq's Democrats," *Wall Street Journal*, October 8, 1991, for background on Charter 91.

and inter-religious conflicts in Iraq and a profound threat to regional and global security.

"Democracy represents a viable future for Iraq. The fear that a democratic Iraq will be taken over by Islamic fundamentalists arises from a lack of understanding of Iraq's political realities and culture. A stable democratic order can be established in Iraq, whose pillars are the Sunni Arabs, Kurds, the significant secular section of the Shi'i population, Christians and Turkomans. Democracy in Iraq is a prerequisite to the rebuilding of the Iraqi economic infrastructure which has been destroyed by decades of economic mismanagement and by the recent conflict in the Gulf. Democracy is needed to facilitate the return of multi-national and foreign companies and capital back into Iraq.

"Peace and security in the region require a peaceful and democratic Iraq. Democracy is an inevitable necessity for maintaining Iraq's integrity and to ensure peaceful coexistence amongst Iraq's various nationalities and religious sects. The new world order requires a democratic Iraq, which can coexist with its neighbors in peace and help the process of economic development and integration in the region.

"Further, the level of cultural and educational development, as well as the devastating experiences associated with dictatorships, will enable Iraqis to practice democracy in a responsible manner. In this regard, Iraq is no less eligible than Jordan, Pakistan or Tunisia.

"However, these historical conditions do not necessarily bring about democracy in Iraq. This raises the question of how to proceed from this point.

"I believe that the Ba'athist dictatorship is not sustainable and is unable to last, owing to the very deep economic, domestic and international problems it is facing. More particularly:

"i)   This dictatorship represents an affront to the new world order;

"ii)   It represents a major threat to regional peace and stability;

"iii)   Most Iraqis are insistent on attaining democracy;

"iv)   There is a strong and relatively well-organized

Kurdish movement which seeks democracy;

"v)   New democratic inclinations have emerged among an increasing number of army officers, who hope to rid Iraq of the current predicament; and

"vi)   the dictatorship has totally failed to realize any of the social, economic or political aspirations of the Iraqi people.

"The possibilities for democratic change are confined to any, or a combination, of the following three scenarios:

"1.   A military coup which may well lead to a period of instability, and perhaps to a succession of coups, but ultimately lead to a democratic order.

"2.   A popular uprising supported by some army divisions and the city of Baghdad.

"3.   Cooperation between the Iraqi opposition and the Kurdish movement, with help from the international community to utilize Kurdistan as a base for democracy in Iraq. A possible scenario will be an armed insurrection with the help of army divisions stationed in the north to help establish a provisional government which may seek international recognition and serve as a catalyst for a wider Iraqi effort to undermine, and ultimately overthrow, dictatorship.

"The Kurdish movement, which is essentially secular and democratic, can play a pivotal role in undermining dictatorship and help formulate a political alternative to the Ba'athist tyranny through cooperation with the Iraqi armed forces and opposition. The Kurdish movement aims at attaining a democratic order in Iraq within which the right of the Kurds to autonomy is recognized. Our commitment to democracy arises from the knowledge that it is the only guarantee for Kurdish rights and a safeguard to prevent a genocide of our people.

"Democracy to us is the panacea for all the problems in Iraq, including the Kurdish problem, and will help us overcome the legacies of repression, deportation and genocide. I can see no future for Iraq but democracy as a prerequisite for enhancing its integrity, unity and viability as a state.

"The Kurdish movement is struggling for such a

democratic order in Iraq and I believe it deserves the active support of the international community."[1]

Dr. Laith Kubba, Executive Committee Member of the INC, Address to National Endowment for Democracy, Washington, July 30, 1992

"What do we propose for the future of Iraq in order to make the democratic experience a success? First, I advocate a decentralization of power. This might weaken the state but it will save the country. I do not advocate decentralization of power based on ethnicity but on regions. I believe by decentralizing power we will reassure those parts of the country that have been repressed for so long. They have lost confidence in the central government and the only way to bring them back into the fold is to allow them to have their own local governments, full expression of cultural rights and to manage their affairs in the way they see fit. In the long run, this will enhance national unity rather than weaken it.

"A second important measure is that political representation should be based on proportional representation and not on a simple majority domination. A third measure is to engage the country immediately in economic reform. Investments need to be made in the parts of the country that have suffered the most. Without a broad economic base for the country, a democratic election alone will not feed hungry stomachs or create stability.

"Lastly, we need to have organizations that will act as watchdogs and observe the overall process and behavior of the government. There is no harm at all in those agencies being international as well as local. I think their presence will encourage democratic process in the country."[2]

---

[1]   *Iraqi Issues*, Vol. 1, No. 1, May 1992.

[2]   *Iraqi Issues*, Vol. 1, No. 4, September 1992.

Iraqi National Congress General Assembly, Final statement of meeting in Salahuddin, Iraq, October 27-31, 1992

"At the September meetings all parties agreed to unite as a representative alternative for the expression of the Iraqi people's will and to work together to eliminate the dictatorial and oppressive regime. All parties endorsed a democratic, constitutional, parliamentary, federal and pluralist structure for Iraq to eliminate sectarian and racial oppression. All parties also reaffirmed their commitment to the rule of law, human rights, basic freedoms and the faith of the nation embodied in Islam, the state religion, which guides the people with its noble values of forgiveness and generosity.

"Against this background, the Iraqi National Congress [INC] National Assembly convened for five days to discuss the current political situation in Iraq and the region. They stressed that Saddam Hussein's regime must be removed to end Iraq's national tragedy...

"The National Assembly reaffirmed the Kurdish people's right to self-determination within a united and democratic Iraq... The National Assembly discussed the formation of a constitutional federal union as a means of ensuring coexistence between the nationality groupings within the Iraqi homeland. The National Assembly reaffirmed its unfailing commitment to the unity and territorial integrity of Iraq and stressed that the true threat to Iraq's unity comes from the dictatorial regime's attempt to divide the people.

"The National Assembly discussed the democratic experiment that took place in Iraqi Kurdistan and welcomed the election of the Kurdish parliament and government. The delegates considered this experience an important step on the path to broadening and spreading political freedom and democratic processes throughout the Iraqi homeland...

"The National Assembly committed the INC to removing Saddam's regime and ending Iraq's national tragedy. The INC pledges to facilitate the return of all exiled Iraqis and to carry out free elections for a national congress that will establish a permanent constitution, the rule of law, justice and freedom."[1]

Hoshyar Zebari, Address to Center for Strategic and International Studies seminar, Washington, D.C., March 17, 1993

"In May 1992, the Kurdish people undertook to legitimize their status by conducting what many observers have noted as the first free elections in the history of Iraq. I'm not suggesting here that the mere existence of multi-party elections or competition means that you can guarantee genuine democracy. But this is the first step in the right direction which Kurdish people, who are part of the Iraqi people, have taken. The May election proved to all those skeptics that democratic change is possible in Iraq if certain conditions are provided.

"Indeed, the Kurdish leadership took a historical step on the 19th of May by holding free and general elections for the regional constituent assembly and for regional government, filling the legal and administrative vacuum left by the Iraqi government's withdrawal from the region and also to administer the local affairs of the region. The withdrawal of the Iraqi administrative and security forces from the region was followed by an internal economic and administrative blockade to force the population into submission...

"Now, a 105-member Kurdish Assembly is in place, as well as a local government...

"The elections were not only free, but the voting process was unobstructed, orderly and peaceful, with enthusiastic participation by the people. The election campaign, as witnessed by many observers, had the festive feeling of a carnival. It also established the freedom of the press and the freedom of choice. In fact, the election process was commended by human rights and electoral monitors from the United States and many others countries.

---

[1]   *Iraqi Issues*, Vol. 1, No. 5, December 1992.

"Of course, this would not have happened without the coalition's protection, without the security arrangements provided by the coalition forces. And for that, the Kurdish people will be grateful forever...

"The elections were an important step forward for the Kurds, but they have caused no fundamental change and I believe for the near future it will not change the basic parameters of our situation...

"In our view, the situation is only likely to change if a democratic civilian government comes to power in Iraq.

"The single greatest threat to the unity and territorial integrity of Iraq is the dictatorship of Saddam Hussein. Until Saddam's tyranny is replaced by a constitutional, parliamentary and democratic structure, Iraq and its neighbors are at risk from factionalism, conflict and chaos.

"We believe that democracy is the only guarantor of stability for a diverse nation in a volatile region. We are dedicated to the institution of constitutional, democratic and pluralistic government in Iraq, expressed through a federal structure for the Kurdish people within Iraq. We also feel that a strong and democratic central government ensuring essential regional, minority and individual rights will ensure Iraq's internal stability and create unity through diversity. Saddam Hussein is destroying the Iraqi nation by division, oppression and aggression. Only through plans for the implementation of the principles I have mentioned will Iraq's unity and sovereignty be preserved...I believe very strongly that the foreign policy objective of the U.S. toward Iraq should be geared to support democracy and human rights...

"We, in the opposition, have to prove that there is a genuine alternative, there is a democratic alternative to this regime."[1]

---

1   *Iraqi Issues*, Vol. 1, No. 7, April, 1993.

JORDAN

Jordanian National Charter, June 1991

Chapter Two: State Governed by Law and Political Pluralism

First: The State of Law and Political Pluralism

1. The State of Law is a democratic state committed to the principle of the supremacy of the law and derives its legitimacy, authority and effectiveness from the free will of the people and all authorities within it are committed to providing legal, judicial and administrative guarantees to protect the rights, integrity and basic freedoms of the individual which rules were laid down by Islam and confirmed by the Universal Declaration of Human Rights...

2. The Jordanian State is a State of Law in the modern sense of a democratic state. It is a state for all citizens regardless of any differences of opinion or any pluralism of approach. It derives its strength from an actual and declared application of the principles of equality, justice and equal opportunities and from the provision of practical means enabling the Jordanian people to participate in the decisions affecting their lives and their affairs...

Second: Basic Pillars of a State of Law

1. Adherence to the letter and spirit of the constitution by the legislative, executive and judiciary authorities in all their actions, within a framework of priority of the right.

2. Adherence to the principle of the supremacy of the law, within a framework of comprehensive review by an independent judiciary.

3. Adherence, in the exercise of democracy, to the principles and requisites of social justice.

4. Ensuring that laws in general and laws pertaining to political parties, elections and publications in particular are dedicated to safeguarding the citizens' basic rights and public freedoms.

5. Adoption of the democratic dialogue as the basis of expressing the views, free from any form of coercion or intellectual terrorism, at all official and public levels.

6. Adherence by government institutions, in the exercise of their duties and services to the public and entities to the principle of complete equality...

Third: Guarantees of the Democratic Approach

The most important guarantees of the democratic approach and achievement of political pluralism are the adherence to the following principles:

1. Respecting the fundamentals of democratic action by organized political groups and parties in their general conduct since it constitutes a guarantee to justice and stability.

2. Strengthening the traits of tolerance and objectivity, [and] respect for the beliefs of others...

3. Guaranteeing the basic freedoms of all citizens in such a manner as to protect the structure of a democratic society, preserve the rights of individuals and ensure full freedom of expression and its declaration with complete liberty within the limits of the constitution.

4. Attaining equality, justice and equal opportunities for all citizens, male and female, without discrimination.

5. Preserving the civilian and democratic nature of the state...

Fourth: Principles and Limitations Governing the Establishment of Parties

1. Jordanians enjoy the right to establish and belong to political parties and groupings provided that their objectives are legitimate, their methods are peaceful and their statutes do not violate the provisions of the constitution. Laws regulating the operation of parties should not include any provisions which overtly or implicitly call for abrogating the constitutional right to establish political parties.

2. Political and party work in Jordan is based on the principle of pluralism of thought, opinion and organization and on securing the requisites of democratic competition and its legitimate means...

4. The judiciary is solely empowered to decide on any infringement pertaining to the application of the Parties

Law...

5. a. Parties must employ democratic methods in their internal workings, choice of leadership and in the exercise of their activities within a framework of democratic dialogue and free competition among the political parties. The same shall apply to relations and dealings by any party with the other political parties and groupings as well as with popular and constitutional institutions in a spirit of mutual respect for opposing views.

b. There shall be no structural or financial affiliation by the leadership or members of any party with any non-Jordanian. Also, no instructions or directions shall be conducted upon instructions or directions from any foreign state or body... [Activities] of any licensed Jordanian party serving Palestine, Arab unity or Islamic solidarity shall be regarded as a national Jordanian undertaking...

King Hussein bin Talal, Address to conference endorsing the Jordanian National Charter, June 9, 1991

"It was clear to us from the beginning that for democracy to be truly democratic, it must fulfill all its own conditions. These are:

"First, separation of executive, legislative and judicial powers. This is what we have sought, and will continue to seek to entrench in accordance with the regulations of the constitution. Each of the three authorities has to know its limits and not infringe on the domain of the others.

"Second, holding general legislative elections according to law. This is what we did in November 1989, when elections took place in an atmosphere of honesty, freedom and respectable competition.

"Third, exercising national political activities on the basis of pluralism, out of the principle of commitment to responsible dialogue, which constitutes the distinctive characteristic of democratic life, and out of the principle that in a democratic state, the truth is not monopolized by an individual or a group of individuals. In the end, it is the result of national dialogue between the groups, which is called harmony.

"To organize and protect political pluralism, thus protecting democracy, a national charter had to be set to be the intellectual document for reference on Jordanian political activity.

"Therefore, the Royal Commission for Drafting the National Charter was formed on April 9, 1990. The fact that this commission has concluded its work is another broad step down the road of democracy and its goals. Today, we meet to place this draft in your hands; to be more precise, in the hands of our citizens whom you represent by virtue of your positions, and by virtue of their choice of you from among various popular figures which our people are teeming with in all walks of life and on all levels. Our concern was deep and comprehensive that this commission include all our people from the various intellectual and political schools and trends; academic, social and economic figures; nomadic and urban communities; Muslims and Christians; deputies and senate members; women and men...

"We are well advised, then, to make every effort to learn from our experience and the experience of others. We must bear in mind that despotism, isolationism and discord among the various sectors of the society cannot but bring more backwardness, confusion and disintegration. If democracy is to be interpreted as irresponsible freedom or the license to abuse, libel, do injustice, cross the lines separating powers, or as a silk cloak concealing poison daggers, or fishing in troubled waters and laying ambush to the detriment of the general well-being of society, or an umbrella providing cover for intellectual terrorism or a means whereby a larger sector dominates a smaller sector, this would, by God, be chaos, pure and simple, and this would be the Achilles' heel of democracy and the ruin of society and the country.

"A democratic society is one which respects law and order because it has made the law. A democratic society is a society of free but responsible dialogue. A democratic society is one which allows diversity of opinion, on condition that counter-opinion is respected and as long as there is commitment to the general interest. A democratic society is free of ideological terrorism, so that the essence of creativity and invention is not dried up.

"A democratic society is remote from despotism, so that it does not suffer from paralysis among its members. A democratic society is a competitive one; however, it is far-removed from violence, fanaticism, grudges, malice and account-settling.

"In order to protect democracy and political pluralism, and in order to avoid all the pitfalls I have already mentioned, we took this successful step, with God's help, of formulating a National Charter. Nevertheless, I hope we will not cheat ourselves into believing that democracy will be safe and sound as long as we finalize its institutions. The constitution and the National Charter, and the laws and legislation that will emerge from them are all-important pillars in the structure of the state of law and democratic society. However, what is no less important are the citizens themselves in the various positions and institutions, since they are the ones who express democracy in word and deed.

"I have closely watched the course of democratic performance since the 1989 elections. It has been generally satisfactory. In my opinion, this was so because of the novelty of the experiment. Therefore, we are all responsible for rectifying the course until it becomes a part of our life. The responsibility of observing and rectifying is a general responsibility which includes the members of the executive and legislative power and free journalism in particular.

"History tells us that democracy, saturated with grudges, indignation, chaos, anger, almost destroyed its own birthplace, the ancient Greek state of Athens, during its prime. This was the case when democracy was practiced in the age of Pericles with predilections of grudges and account-settling rather than considering the general interest.

"I only say this to assert that we might have to fear for democracy from those who live under its canopy and harm it in the name of democracy itself, wittingly or unwittingly. Democracy is not a mere institution but, rather, a culture and way of life that characterizes a certain human society. This clear reference of mine is to assert that the homeland must come first. Every party that is established under the canopy of democracy and in its name is necessarily a national [watani] party in terms of its bases, objectives, means, funding and connections. Any departure from this reality is not only a departure from democracy but also a departure from the homeland."[1]

King Hussein bin Talal, Interview, May 2, 1993

Question: "Many people still see [Iraq] as a potentially destabilizing factor in this region. What role do you see for Iraq and for Saddam Hussein?"
Hussein: "...I wish for [Iraq] to remain together. Its integrity is important but beyond that I wish for it national reconciliation, real movement towards democracy, pluralism, respect for human rights and hopefully an end to this nightmare of suffering of the Iraqi people themselves..."

Q: "Do you feel democracy is now at the stage it should be at in Jordan?"
Hussein: "Yes, I feel it is despite enormous difficulties, suspicions, hostility by some in the region to the very concept. But it has to happen, it is going to happen everywhere sooner or later.
    "The clock cannot be turned nor can we have a situation where people are denied their basic rights and, thank God, here in Jordan these rights were given because we believed in them and recognized them as such and I would hope certainly that our other brethren in the Arab world can look at this example as a serious and worldly one to look at in terms of shaping the future."

Q: "There seem to be people in Jordan who fear democracy, who worry that the Jordan they know will become fundamentally different. Is democracy irreversible now?"
Hussein: "I believe it is irreversible and obviously there is

---

1   Radio Jordan Network, June 9, 1991, as printed in *FBIS*, June 10.

a danger that democracy will be a threatened democra[tic process] but I don't think this will happen here and my efforts will go towards sharing... the responsibility [the individual voter] has towards himself, towards his country and beyond that to the region itself."[1]

KUWAIT

Prime Minister Abdallah al-Salim al-Sabah, Interview in Sawt al-Kuwait, September 19, 1992

"Any Kuwaiti who finds the capability in himself and who meets the conditions for candidacy will find the door open to him to serve his homeland. In this connection we do not differentiate among them or set conditions other than those known to everyone. The arena is open to all. It concerns me as a citizen and official that the upcoming elections should be held in a friendly and brotherly atmosphere and that everyone should adopt the slogan 'always in the service of Kuwait.'...

"Everyone must fight the election process in accordance with the stipulations of the election law. I realize that a number of observers and reporters from all over the world will be coming to Kuwait to cover the election process. And I hope that the candidates in particular and citizens in general will ensure that this process, which we care about, is conducted in an atmosphere of security and that a spirit of brotherhood and sound democratic competitiveness will prevail among all, as we have always experienced in Kuwait."[2]

Prime Minister Abdallah al-Salim al-Sabah, Interview, October 3, 1992

Question: "Does Your Highness think the realization of the

---

[1]   *Jordan Times*, May 2, 1993, as printed in *FBIS*, May 3.
[2]   *Sawt al-Kuwayt al-Duwali*, September 19, 1992, as printed in *FBIS*, September 23.

democratic process in Kuwait warrants the widening of the electorate and popular participation through the participation of many Kuwaitis who are not allowed at the moment to vote? If so, what is the government's [view] on those problems facing the realization of such an aim, particularly today when there is so much talk about the woman's right to vote, the right of naturalized people to vote and the lowering of the legal age to vote to eighteen in a bid to broaden popular participation in Kuwait?"

Al-Sabah: "I am for this idea that is aimed at widening the participation of the electorate. Everybody who has been following the amir's speeches, may God protect him, before and after the liberation can see that His Highness had pointed out clearly and unequivocally the need for widening popular participation, particularly the role of the Kuwaiti sister, who stood by the side of her brother, condemned the Iraqi aggression against Kuwait, rejected and denounced the Iraqi occupation of Kuwait and cooperated with her brother in all fields, subjecting herself to investigation, torture, violence and death. Despite all this, she, the Kuwaiti sister—the sister, the mother, the wife and the daughter—stood fast. And we are all appreciative of her role, which was a loyal and heroic one.

"Therefore, the subject of giving her the right to political participation is in my opinion a matter— notwithstanding the various opinions that I have heard during the election campaign, some of which were for, some of which had reservations and others thought despite the importance of such a matter it should be contemplated in due course in the future...However, this matter should be above all that. I am certain that this matter will be discussed by brother members of the next National Council. It is my opinion, however, that the next National Council will give full consideration to all factors as well as full appreciation and recognition of women's role."[1]

---

[1] KSC Television, October 3, 1992, as printed in *FBIS*, October 5.

Jasim Hamad al-Saqr, National Assembly member, Address, October 20, 1992

"National unity prevails as a result of justice; it flourishes as a result of equality and equal opportunities; it becomes stronger as a result of the expansion and deepening of popular participation. It ultimately imposes on the representatives of the people that they be a model in overlooking personal interests and political gain, and to be an example in discarding tribal fanaticism and sectarian favoritism so that the interests of Kuwait alone will be the basis of their debate and the aim of their decision. The political mission of our assembly is manifested in its historic responsibility for spreading true democracy and for encouraging everyone to practice it, and to remove fears that this true democracy may stumble throughout our Arab and Islamic nation, because in democracy lies the strength and success of this nation and the correctness of its course.

"In popular participation and consultation lies what prevents the adventures of tyrants who violate the dignity of peoples, shed their blood and destroy the edifices of states and their values. In order that our assembly may carry out its mission, it should prove the ability of consultation and popular participation to build homelands and deal with the problems of citizens. It should also reaffirm that democracy bolsters national unity and does not weaken it, and guarantees the correctness of decisions and does not misinterpret them, and balances between aspirations and capabilities and does not leap over them."[1]

LEBANON

The Ta'if Accords (The Lebanese National Accord), October 23, 1989

I.   *General Principles*
A.   Lebanon is sovereign, free and independent country and

---

[1]   Radio Kuwait, October 20, 1992, as printed in *FBIS*, October 21.

a final homeland for all its citizens.

B. Lebanon is Arab in belonging and identity. It is an active and founding member of the Arab League and is committed to the league's charters. It is an active and founding member of the United Nations Organization and is committed to its charters. Lebanon is a member of the nonaligned movement. The state of Lebanon shall embody these principles in all areas and spheres, without exception.

C. Lebanon is democratic parliamentary republic founded on respect for public liberties, especially the freedom of expression and belief, on social justice and on equality in rights and duties among all citizens, without discrimination or preference.

D. The people are the source of authority. They are sovereign and they shall exercise their sovereignty through the constitutional institutions.

E. The economic system is a free system that guarantees individual initiative and private ownership.

E. (*sic*)Culturally, socially and economically-balanced development is a mainstay of the state's unity and of the system's stability.

F. Efforts to achieve comprehensive social justice through fiscal, economic and social reform.

G. Lebanon's soil is united and it belongs to all the Lebanese. Every Lebanese is entitled to live in and enjoy any part of the country under the supremacy of the law. The people may not be categorized on the basis of any affiliation whatsoever and there shall be no fragmentation, no partition and no repatriation [of Palestinians in Lebanon].

H. No authority violating the common coexistence

charter shall be legitimate.

II. *Political Reforms*

A. Chamber of Deputies: The Chamber of Deputies is the legislative authority which exercises full control over government policy and activities...

6. The number of members of the Chamber of Deputies shall be increased to 108, shared equally by Christians and Muslims. As for the districts created on the basis of this document and the districts whose seats became vacant prior to the proclamation of this document, their seats shall be filled only once on an emergency basis through appointment by the national accord government that is planned to be formed.

7. With the election of the first Chamber of Deputies on a national, not sectarian, basis, a senate shall be formed and all the spiritual families shall be represented in it. The senate powers shall be confined to crucial issues...

B. President of Republic: The president of the republic is the head of state and the symbol of the country's unity. He shall contribute to enhancing the constitution and to preserving Lebanon's independence, unity and territorial integrity in accordance with the provisions of the constitution. He is the supreme commander of the armed forces which are subject to the power of the cabinet. The president shall exercise the following powers.

1. Head the cabinet [meeting] whenever he wishes, but without voting.

2. Head the Supreme Defense Council.

3. Issue decrees and demand their publication. He shall also be entitled to ask the cabinet to reconsider any resolution it makes within fifteen days of the date of deposition of the resolution with the presidential office...

G. Abolition of Political Sectarianism: Abolishing political sectarianism is a fundamental national objective. To achieve it, it is required that efforts be made in accordance with a phased plan. The Chamber of Deputies elected on the basis of equal sharing by Christians and

Muslims shall adopt the proper measures to achieve this objective and to form a national council which is headed by the president of the republic and which includes, in addition to the prime minister and the Chamber of Deputies speaker, political, intellectual and social notables. The council's task will be to examine and propose the means capable of abolishing sectarianism, to present them to the Chamber of Deputies and the cabinet and to observe implementation of the phased plan. The following shall be done in the interim period:

a. Abolish the sectarian representation base and rely on capability and specialization in public jobs, the judiciary, the military, security, public and joint institutions, and in the independent agencies in accordance with the dictates of national accord, excluding the top-level jobs and equivalent jobs which shall be shared equally by Christians and Muslims without allocating any particular job to any sect.

b. Abolish the mention of sect and denomination on the identity card.

III. *Other Reforms*
A. Administrative Decentralism:

1. The state of Lebanon shall be single and united state with a strong central authority.

2. The powers of the governors and district administrative officers shall be expanded and all state administrations shall be represented in the administrative provinces at the highest level possible so as to facilitate serving the citizens and meeting their needs locally.

3. The administrative division shall be reconsidered in a manner that emphasizes national fusion within the framework of preserving common coexistence and unity of the soil, people and institutions.

4. Expanded administrative decentralism shall be adopted at the level of the smaller administrative units (district and smaller units) through the election of a council, headed by the district officer, in every district, to insure local participation.

5. A comprehensive and unified development plan

capable of developing the provinces economically and socially shall be adopted and the resources of the municipalities, unified municipalities and municipal unions shall be reinforced with the necessary financial resources...

B.   Spreading the sovereignty of the state of Lebanon over all Lebanese territories: Considering that all Lebanese factions have agreed to the establishment of a strong state founded on the basis of national accord, the national accord government shall draft a detailed one-year plan whose objective is to spread the sovereignty of the state of Lebanon over all Lebanese territories gradually with the state's own forces. The broad lines of the plan shall be as follows:

1.   Disbanding of all Lebanese and non-Lebanese militias shall be announced, the militias' weapons shall be delivered to the state of Lebanon within a period of six months, beginning with the approval of the national accord charter; the president of the republic shall be elected; a national accord cabinet shall be formed; and the political reforms shall be approved constitutionally.

2.   The internal security forces shall be strengthened through:

a.   Opening the door of voluntarism to all the Lebanese without exception, beginning the training of volunteers centrally, distributing the volunteers to the units in the governorates and subjecting them to organized periodic training courses.

b.   Strengthening the security agency to insure control over the entry and departure of individuals into and out of the country by land, air and sea.

3.   Strengthening the armed forces:

a.   The fundamental task of the armed forces is to defend the homeland, and if necessary, protect public order when the danger exceeds the capability of the internal security forces to deal with such a danger on their own.

b.   The armed forces shall be used to support the internal security forces in preserving security under conditions determined by the cabinet.

c. The armed forces shall be unified, prepared and trained in order that they may be able to shoulder their national responsibilities in confronting Israeli aggression.

d. When the internal security forces become ready to assume their security tasks, the armed forces shall return to their barracks.

e. The armed forces intelligence shall be reorganized to serve military objectives exclusively.

4. The problem of the Lebanese evacuees shall be solved fundamentally, and the right of every Lebanese evicted since 1975 to return to the place from which he was evicted shall be established. Legislation to guarantee this right and to insure the means of reconstruction shall be issued. Considering that the objective of the state of Lebanon is to spread its authority over all the Lebanese territories through its own forces, represented primarily by the internal security forces, and in view of the fraternal relations binding Syria to Lebanon, the Syrian forces shall thankfully assist the forces of the legitimate Lebanese government to spread the authority of the state of Lebanon within a set period of no more than two years, beginning with ratification of the national accord charter, election of the president of the republic, formation of the national accord cabinet, and approval of the political reforms constitutionally. At the end of this period, the two governments—the Syrian Government and the Lebanese national accord government—shall decide to redeploy the Syrian forces in al-Biqa' area from Dahr al-Baydar to the Hammana-al-Judayriy-'Ayn Darah line, and if necessary, at other points to be determined by a joint Lebanese-Syrian military committee. An agreement shall also be concluded by the two governments to determine the strength and duration of the presence of Syrian forces in the above-mentioned areas and to define these forces' relationship with the Lebanese state authorities where the forces exist. The Arab Tripartite Committee is prepared to assist the two states, if they so wish, to develop this agreement...

3. Liberating Lebanon from the Israeli occupation: Regaining state authority over the territories extending to

the internationally-recognized Lebanese borders requires the following:

A. Efforts to implement resolution 425 and the other UN Security Council resolution calling for fully eliminating the Israeli occupation.

B. Adherence to the truce agreement concluded on March 23, 1949.

C. Taking all the steps necessary to liberate all Lebanese territories from the Israeli occupation, to spread state sovereignty over all the territories, and to deploy the Lebanese army in the border area adjacent to Israel; and making efforts to reinforce the presence of the UN forces in South Lebanon to insure the Israeli withdrawal and to provide the opportunity for the return of security and stability to the border area.

4. Lebanese-Syrian Relations: Lebanon, with its Arab identity, is tied to all the Arab countries by true fraternal relations. Between Lebanon and Syria there is a special relationship that derives its strength from the roots of blood relationships, history and joint fraternal interests. This is the concept on which the countries' coordination and cooperation is founded, and which will be embodied by the agreements between the two countries in all areas, in a manner that accomplishes the two fraternal countries' interests within the framework of the sovereignty and independence of each of them. Therefore, and because strengthening the bases of security creates the climate needed to develop these special bonds, Lebanon should not be allowed to constitute a source of threat to Syria's security, and Syria should not be allowed to constitute a source of threat to Lebanon's security under any circumstances. Consequently, Lebanon should not allow itself to become a pathway or a base for any force, state or organization seeking to undermine its security or Syria's security. Syria, which is eager for Lebanon's security, independence, and unity, and for harmony among its citizens, should not permit any act that poses a threat to

Lebanon's security, independence and sovereignty.[1]

Lebanese-Syrian Treaty of Brotherhood, Cooperation And Coordination, May 23, 1991

The Lebanese Republic and the Syrian Arab Republic, on the basis of the distinguished brotherly relations between them which derive their strength from the roots of kinship, history, common affiliation, common destiny and joint strategic interests; out of their belief that the achievement of the broadest cooperation and coordination between them will serve their strategic interests and provide the means for ensuring their development and progress and for defending their pan-Arab and national security, be a source of prosperity and stability, enable them to face all regional and international developments, and meet the aspirations of the peoples of the two countries; and in implementation of the Lebanese national accord which was ratified by the Lebanese Chamber of Deputies on November 5, 1989, have agreed on the following:

Article 1
The two states will work to achieve the highest level of cooperation and coordination in all political, economic, security, cultural, scientific and other fields in a manner that will realize the interests of the two fraternal countries within the framework of respect for their individual sovereignty and independence and will enable the two countries to use their political, economic and security resources to provide prosperity and stability, ensure their pan-Arab and national security and expand and strengthen their common interests, as an affirmation of the brotherly relations and guarantee of their common destiny.

---

1   Riyadh Domestic Service, October 22, 1989, as printed in *FBIS*, October 24.

Article 2
The two states will work to achieve cooperation and coordination in the economic, agricultural, industrial and commercial fields, as well as in the fields of transportation, communications, customs, the establishment of joint projects and coordination of development plans.

Article 3
The connection between the security of the two countries requires that Lebanon not become a threat to Syria's security and vice versa under any circumstances. Therefore, Lebanon will not allow itself to become a transit point or base for any force, state or organization that seeks to undermine its security, independence and unity, and the agreement among its people, will not allow any action that threatens Lebanon's security, independence and sovereignty.

Article 4
After the political reforms are approved in a constitutional manner, as stipulated in the Lebanese national accord, and after the deadlines specified in this accord have expired, the Syrian and Lebanese Governments will decide on the redeployment of the Syrian forces in the al-Biqa' area and the entrance to western al-Biqa' in Dahr al-Baydar up to Hammanah-al-Mudayrij-'Ayn Dara line, and if necessary in other points to be specified by a joint Lebanese-Syrian military committee. The two governments will conclude an agreement specifying the size and duration of the Syrian forces' presence in these areas and the relationship of these forces with the authorities of the Lebanese state.

Article 5
The two states' Arab and international foreign policies shall be based on the following principles:
  1. Lebanon and Syria are Arab states which are committed to the Arab League Charter, the Arab defense pact and joint economic cooperation, and all agreements ratified within the framework of the Arab League. They are members of the United Nations and are committed to its

charter. They are also members of the Nonaligned Movement.

2. The two countries share a common destiny and common interests.

3. Each country supports the other in issues related to its security and national interests in accordance of the contents of this treaty. Therefore, the governments of the two countries shall coordinate their Arab and international policies, cooperate to the fullest extent possible in Arab and international institutions and organizations and coordinate their stands on regional and international issues.

Article 6
The following bodies shall be formed to achieve the goals of this treaty. Other bodies can be established by a decision from the Supreme Council.

1. *The Supreme Council:*

A. The Supreme Council will consist of the presidents of the two contracting countries and a number of other members from both countries.

B. The Supreme Council will meet at least once a year, and more often when necessary, at a venue to be agreed upon.

C. The Supreme Council charts the general policy for coordination and cooperation between the two states in the political, economic, security, military and other fields. It also supervises the implementation of this policy and adopts the plans and decisions that are made by the executive body, the foreign affairs committee, the economic and social affairs committee, the defense and security affairs committee or any committee that is established in the future, provided that the constitutional provisions of the two countries are respected.

D. The Supreme Council's decisions are binding and effective within the framework of the constitutional laws and rules of the two countries, except for those decisions which require the approval of the executive or legislative authority in the two countries under their constitutional provisions.

E. The Supreme Council defines the subjects on which

the committees concerned have the right to make decisions. Once they are issued, these decisions assume an executive nature within the framework of the constitutional laws and rules of the two countries, except for those decisions which require the approval of the executive or legislative authorities in the two countries under their constitutional provisions...[1]

Draft Electoral Law (summary), June 16, 1992

The following are the bill's most important points:
1. There are 128 deputies.
2. Electoral constituencies: The Governorates in Beirut, the south, and the north. In al-Biqa' and the mountain, the District.
3. The sectarian and factional distribution of seats: Some 27 for the Sunni, 27 for the Shi'a, 34 for the Maronites, 8 for the Druze, 8 for the Greek Catholics, 14 for the Greek Orthodox, 2 for the Alawites, 1 for the Anglicans, 1 for the Armenian Catholics, 5 for the Armenian Orthodox and 1 for the other Christian minorities.[2]

General Hasan Nasrallah, Secretary General of Hezbollah, News conference, June 30, 1992

"We fully support holding parliamentary elections as soon as possible so that the Lebanese people will be able to freely choose their representatives. Second, in view of the fact that Hezbollah represents a popular support and a surging element of motivation; in an endeavor to benefit from all positions to channel the political arena toward activating the resistance option; to promote our contribution to the defense of the oppressed and the deprived and to

---

[1]   Voice of Lebanon Radio, May 17, 1991, as printed in *FBIS*, May 20, 1991.
[2]   *al-Safir*, July 17, 1992, as printed in *FBIS*, July 23, 1992. The full text, including the breakdown of parliamentary districts by sect, is reproduced in *al-Safir*, June 16, 1992, and printed in *FBIS*, July 16.

adopt their causes; to contribute towards the serious endeavor to eliminate political sectarianism, the root of evil and corruption in this country; and to get a Chamber of Deputies that can deal with this stage and its great challenges: We declare that we decided to participate in the upcoming electoral process. We do this with the hope that the active and good forces will have a chance to express themselves and the extent of their support freely and honestly."[1]

General Hasan Nasrallah, Secretary General of Hezbollah, Interview in al-Nahar, September 3, 1992

Question: "Don't you fear a repetition of the Algerian experience here?"
Nasrallah: "There is a great difference between Lebanon and Algeria. The Algerian regime's problem was the Islamists' sweep of the parliament. They got more than two-thirds of the seats, which would have enabled them to change the nation's character. The structure in Lebanon, the variety here and the distribution of parliamentary seats means that the situation is not comparable. Consequently, I do not believe that our party's entry into the Chamber of Deputies, regardless of the numbers, should create fears similar to those of the Algerian regime... Our presence in the Chamber of Deputies will give it an additional boost that will enable it to assume its important and pivotal role in Lebanon's political life. There is no need to deal with Hezbollah's victory in the same way the Islamists' victory in Algeria was dealt with...

"Our election program... is one of action, not of propaganda... We have never been a military party or a militia. We presented ourselves as a *jihad* movement to confront the continued occupation and aggression against our people and our territories. Our participation in the Chamber of Deputies absolutely does not negate the fact that we are a resistance movement. The reasons and

---

[1]   Voice of Lebanon Radio, June 30, 1992, as printed in *FBIS*, June 30.

motives that move people, or an entire people, to engage in resistance activity still exist; that is, the continued occupation."[1]

General Hasan Nasrallah, Secretary General of Hezbollah, Interview in Resalat, October 13, 1992

Question: "Why did you decide to start political activities?"

Nasrallah: "Since its formation, Hezbollah has been involved in political activities... Our participation in parliament is new... That Hezbollah participated in the elections and entered parliament can be said to be a new issue, but we should not forget that for the past twenty years, parliamentary elections were not held in Lebanon. Had these elections been held five years ago, we would also have participated then. In short, we do not accept the belief that our military struggle has entered a political phase. From the start we had political activities, but the major part of our activities is and will be the *jihad* movement... This is our principle and we will not retreat from it..."

Q: "Now that Hezbollah deputies have entered the Lebanese Parliament, what is your future strategy in the country?"

Nasrallah: "The deputies must operate on three pivots. The first is resistance, political effort, propaganda and assisting the government in every field, especially in helping the people who are living in war-stricken areas... Another political mission for our deputies is to confront the idea of talks with Israel and we should strive so that the other deputies will also be convinced these talks are wrong. Peace with this cancerous tumor is wrong and dangerous and we should say that the threat of peace is more than the threat of war with the Zionists. In parliament we will challenge the talks with Israel.

---

1   *Al-Nahar*, August 25, 1992, as printed in *FBIS*, September 3.

"The second pivot is based of denominationalism existing in the Lebanese system and government positions being distributed on its basis. For example, the president should be Christian, the prime minister Sunni, and the speaker Shi'i. Based on the constitution, parliament has the right to cancel this denominationalism. We are seriously pursuing this issue, because the main reason behind the political, social and economic corruption in Lebanon is this political denominationalism that we are trying to end.

"The third pivot is that our efforts aim to make laws to serve the oppressed and the deprived, confronting laws that are against the interests of the oppressed, especially since laws have been approved in Lebanon that support the capitalists' interests. Generally speaking, we are trying to improve the people's economic and social situation."[1]

Prime Minister Rafiq Hariri, Address, November 2, 1992

"Every member of this government is a minister for all of Lebanon, not for a sect or an area. We want this to be a new stage in the life of the country and the people. We want the coming period to witness years of hope, reassurance and stability, leading to self-sufficiency and prosperity. We want to see every displaced person return to his house and land. We want to see our emigrant brothers and sons return to their homeland to participate in its building.

"Much has been achieved through the national reconciliation agreement. We want this government to follow the same course, reinforcing what has been achieved and developing the Lebanese democratic system and the free Lebanese economy. We want the national march to proceed with a spirit of reconciliation acceptable to the citizens and supported by the great majority of them. This majority should be vocal, active and demonstrate initiative, directing our march in the right way to help us

---

[1]   *Resalat*, October 13, 1992, as printed in *FBIS*, October 28.

overcome the years of strife."[1]

SAUDI ARABIA

The "Secular" Petition, December 1990. Drafted in the fall of 1990, this petition, signed by forty-three public figures, including cabinet ministers, businessmen and professors, was a moderate call for reform that sought to avoid association with any radical political groups.

1. A systematic framework for *fatwa*. It must take into consideration the *sharia*, which is infallible and unchangeable, as represented in the unequivocal texts of the Koran and the Hadith. But jurisprudence commentaries, Koran interpreters' views and the opinions of *sharia* experts that are derived from divergent scholarly doctrines are all human attempts to comprehend the *sharia* texts. These views are affected by their authors' ability to understand, given their level of knowledge and skill.. Shaped by the circumstances of time and place, these views are liable to be wrong as well as right, and should be subject to debate. Indeed, there has been a consensus among scholars that no one may ever claim the sole right to determine the meaning of the Koran or the Hadith or monopolize the right to decide *sharia* rules. It is therefore essential that we clearly and forcefully make a distinction between what is divine and what is human. The revealed and unambiguous texts must be accepted and obeyed. But scholarly opinions may be freely examined and questioned without any limits.
2. Consider issuing a basic law of government in light of the statements and declarations made by the rulers of the country at various times.

3. Formation of a consultative council comprising the elite from among the qualified and knowledgeable opinion makers known for their honesty, forthrightness,

---

[1]   Radio Lebanon, November 2, 1992, as printed in *FBIS*, November 2.

impartiality, morality and public service, representing all regions of the kingdom. The council must have among its responsibilities the study, development and adoption of laws and rules related to all economic, political, educational and other issues and should exercise effective scrutiny of all executive agencies.

4. The revival of municipal councils; the implementation of the Law of Provinces; and the generalization of the chamber of commerce experience as a model for all other trades.

5. The investigation of all aspects of the judicial system, in all its degrees, types and areas of competence, for the purpose of modernizing its laws and evaluating the process of preparing judges and their assistants. Every step necessary must be taken to guarantee independence of the judiciary, to assure its effectiveness and fairness, spread its authority and strengthen its foundations. Schools that train for this important field must be open to all citizens, not reserved to one group over the others in violation of the *sharia*-based principle of equality of opportunity.

6. Commitment to total equality among all citizens in all aspects of their life, without distinction based on ethnic, tribal, sectarian or social origins. The principle of protecting citizens against interference in their lives except by a court order must be firmly established.

7. Media policy must be reviewed and set according to a comprehensive and precise law reflecting the most advanced legislation in other countries. This law must enable all Saudi media to exercise their freedom in preaching good over evil, calling for virtue and shunning vice, enabling dialogue in an open Muslim society.

8. Comprehensive reform of the Associations for the Propagation of Virtue and the Deterrence of Vice. A precise law must be adopted specifying their functions and the method they must follow, and setting strict rules for hiring

chiefs and members of precincts, to ensure judicious and tactful preaching.

9.   Although we believe that nurturing the new generation is the highest duty of Muslim women, we nevertheless believe that there are numerous fields of public life where women can be allowed to participate—within the scope of the *sharia*—thus honoring them and acknowledging their role in building society.

10. God revealed His holy books, and sent His prophets, to educate and nurture humanity, proving that education is the foremost important basis for the renaissance and progress of nations. We believe that our country's educational system is in need of comprehensive and fundamental reform to enable it to graduate faithful generations that are qualified to contribute positively and effectively in building the present and the future of the country, and to face the challenges of the age, enabling us to catch up with the caravan of nations that have vastly surpassed us in every field.[1]

The "Religious" Petition, February 1991. This petition, a response to the popularity of the "secular" petition, was signed by many top members of the religious establishment in Saudi Arabia.

"In this critical period, everybody has recognized the need for change. We therefore find that the most requisite duty is to reform our present conditions that have caused us to suffer these tribulations. Consequently, we ask that the ruler of the nation check the deterioration of these conditions, which need reform in the following areas:

---

[1]   Aziz Abu-Hamad, *Empty Reforms: Saudi Arabia's New Basic Laws* (Washington, D.C.: Middle East Watch, 1992). In the preamble, the forty-three signatories, both secular and religious, declared their devotion to the king and "the present system of government, and to preserving the cherished royal family" before listing their proposed reforms.

1. The formation of a consultative council to decide internal and external issues on the basis of the *sharia*. Its members must be honest, straightforward and representing all fields of expertise. They must be totally independent and not be subject to any pressure that may affect the authority of the council.

2. All laws and regulations of political, economic, administrative or other nature must be reconciled with the principles of the *sharia*. Trusted committees with expertise in *sharia* should be authorized to repeal legislation not conforming to *sharia* principles.

3. In addition to possessing specialized expertise, dedication and honesty, government officials and their overseas representatives must be unswervingly moral. Failing any one of these requirements for any reason is an abuse of public trust and a fundamental cause of injury to the national interest and reputation.

4. Justice must be applied, rights granted and duties assigned in full equality among all citizens, not favoring the nobles or begrudging the weak. Abuse of authority by anyone whether by shirking obligations or denying people what is their right is a cause for the breakup and annihilation of society.

5. All government officials, especially those occupying the highest positions, must be diligently scrutinized and must be made accountable with no exceptions. Government agencies must be cleansed of anyone whose corruption or dereliction is proven, regardless of any other consideration.

6. Public wealth must be distributed fairly among all classes and groups. Taxes must be eliminated and fees that have overburdened citizens must be reduced. Government revenues must be protected from exploitation and abuse; priority in expenditure must be given to the most urgent necessities. All forms of monopoly or illegitimate ownership must be eliminated. Restrictions imposed on

Islamic banks must be lifted. Public and private banking institutions must be cleansed of usury, which is an affront to God and His Prophet, and a cause for stunting the growth of wealth.

7.   A strong and fully-integrated army must be built and fully-equipped with weapons of all kinds, from any source. Attention must be given to manufacturing and developing arms. The goal of the army must be to protect the country and the holy sites.

8.   Information media must be remodeled according to the adopted media policy of the kingdom. The goals must be to educate, serve Islam and express the morals of society. The media must be purged of anything conflicting with these objectives. Its freedom to spread awareness through truthful reporting and constructive criticism must be safeguarded within the confines of Islam.

9.   Foreign policy must be based on national interest without relying on alliances not sanctioned by the *sharia*. It must also embrace Muslim causes. The kingdom's embassies must be reformed to enable them to reflect the Islamic nature of the country.

10. Religious and proselytizing institutions must be developed and strengthened with financial and human resources. All obstacles preventing them from fully carrying out their objectives must be removed.

11. Judicial institutions must be unified and granted full and effective independence. Juridical authority must apply to all. It is necessary to establish an independent body whose function is to ensure carrying out judicial orders.

12. The rights of individuals and society must be guaranteed. Every restriction on people's rights and their will must be removed, to ensure the enjoyment of human

dignity, within the acceptable religious safeguards.[1]

King Fahd ibn Abd al-Aziz, Interview in al-Siyassah, *March 30, 1992*

Question: "What about the new laws of government which were announced in... the Kingdom of Saudi Arabia. It is said that they were formulated late and were promulgated under international pressure."
Fahd: "These laws could have come earlier, and I spoke about them to the Saudi people. But the events in the region led to the delay in issuing them. They stem from the Islamic *sharia*, which is the original source. To say that they are the result of pressure from this or that side is nothing but hearsay and has no basis in truth or reality. Those who say such a thing know nothing about the reality and genuineness of the Saudi people and know nothing about the true character of this society and its structure, roots and traditions. The Saudi people are capable of respecting their traditions and conventions and Arab roots...
"Saudi Arabia and its people are not things which learn lessons or submit to pressure from anyone [as received]. This is because we respect the affairs of others and do not interfere with them; likewise, we expect others to respect us as we respect them. The three laws stem from a Saudi visualization and from our true traditions."

Q: "What do you think of the democratic systems which prevail in the world? Is the system of free elections suitable for our peoples here?"
Fahd: "The prevailing democratic system in the world is not suitable for us in this region, for our peoples' composition and traits are different from the traits of that world. We cannot import the way in which other peoples deal (with their own affairs) in order to apply it on our people; we have our own Muslim faith which is a complete system and a complete religion.

---

[1]   Aziz Abu-Hamad, *Empty Reforms: Saudi Arabia's New Basic Laws* (Washington, D.C.: Middle East Watch, 1992).

"Elections do no fall within the sphere of the Muslim religion, which believes in the *al-shurah* (consultative) system and openness between ruler and his subjects and which makes whoever is in charge fully answerable to his people. This does not mean, however, that we should not benefit from the realities brought about by social transformations and any other developments. Nevertheless, any change must (conform) with the teachings of our Muslim faith. Free elections are not suitable for our country, the Kingdom of Saudi Arabia. Our country is a special one, a matter which one should understand; it is the country which is in charge of the two holy mosques on behalf of the Islamic world. This is a country whose political life has been characterized by stability and safety, and by the application of the teachings of Islam. It is therefore a special country."

Q: "You have asserted that free elections are not suitable for your country and the fact that democracy as it is understood in the West also is not suitable."
Fahd: "Of course, we do not interfere in others' internal affairs; the kingdom has been from the outset eager not to interfere in others' (internal affairs) and in their political practices.

"Of course, in my opinion Western democracies could be suitable in their countries but they are not suitable for all the peoples of the world. As I have said, there is no harm in benefiting from some of the good aspects on the condition that those do not disagree with the teachings of our religion."

Q: "Do you think that the Saudi system is suitable for other countries in the region and that they can benefit from it?"
Fahd: "The system of government here has become public and anyone can observe its effectiveness."[1]

---

[1]   Saudi Press Agency (SPA), March 28, 1992, as printed in *FBIS*, March 30.

Basic Law of Government, March 1992

Chapter One: General Principles
Article 1
    The Kingdom of Saudi Arabia is a sovereign Arab Islamic state with Islam as its religion; God's book, and the Sunna of his Prophet, God's prayers and peace be upon him, are its constitution; Arabic is its language; and Riyadh is its capital.

Chapter Two: Law of Government
Article 5
a. The law of government in the Kingdom of Saudi Arabia is monarchy.
c. The king chooses the heir apparent and relieves him by royal order.
e. The heir apparent assumes the powers of the king on the latter's death until the act of allegiance has been carried out.
Article 6
    Citizens are to pay allegiance to the king in accordance with the holy Koran and the Prophet's tradition, in submission and obedience and in times of ease and difficulty, fortune and adversity.
Article 8
    The Government of the Kingdom of Saudi Arabia stands on the bases of justice, *shura* [consultation] and equality in accordance with the Islamic *sharia*.

Chapter Three: Constituents of the Saudi Family
Article 13
    Education will aim at instilling the Islamic faith in the young generation, to provide them with knowledge and skills and to prepare them to become useful members in the building of their society, members who love their homeland and are proud of its history.

Chapter Four: Economic Principles
Article 18
    The state protects the freedom of private property and

its sanctity. No one is to be stripped of his property except when this serves public interest, in which case fair compensation is due.

Chapter Five: Rights and Duties
Article 23

The state protects Islam; it implements its *sharia*; it orders people to do right and to shun evil; it fulfills the duty regarding God's call.

Article 25

The state strives to attain the hopes of the Arab and Islamic nation for solidarity and unity of word and to consolidate its relations with friendly states.

Article 26

The state protects human rights in accordance with the Islamic *sharia*.

Article 27

The state guarantees the right of the citizen and his family in cases of emergency, illness, disability and old age. It supports the system of social security and encourages institutions and persons to contribute acts of charity.

Article 28

The state provides job opportunities to whomever is capable of carrying out such jobs; it enacts laws that protect the employee and the employer.

Article 29

The state guards science, literature and culture; it encourages scientific research; it protects the Islamic and Arab heritage and contributes to Arab, Islamic and human civilization.

Article 34

The defense of the Islamic religion, society and the country is the duty of each citizen. The regime explains the provision of the military service.

Article 36

...No one shall be arrested, imprisoned, or have his actions restricted except in accordance with the provisions of the law.

Article 37

Houses shall have their sanctity and shall not be entered without the permission of their owners or be searched except in cases specified by statutes.

Article 38

...There shall be no crime or penalty except in accordance with religious law [*sharia*] or organizational law [*nizami*].

Chapter Six: Authorities of the State
Article 44

The authorities of the state consist of the following:

a. The judicial authority
b. The executive authority
c. The regulatory authority

These authorities will cooperate with each other in the performance of their duties in accordance with this and other laws. The king shall be the point of reference for all these authorities.

Article 46

The judiciary is an independent authority... there is no hegemony over judges in the dispensation of their judgment except for that of the Islamic *sharia*.

Article 47

The right to litigate is ensured for citizens and residents in the kingdom on an equal basis. The law defines the required procedures for this.

Article 48

The courts will apply the rules of Islamic *sharia* to the cases that are brought before them...

Article 55

The king carries out the policy of the nation, a legitimate policy in accordance with the provisions of Islam; the king oversees the implementation of the Islamic *sharia*, the systems, the state's general policies and the protection and defense of the country.

Article 68

A consultative council is to be created. Its statute will show how it is formed, how it exercises its powers and how its members are selected. The king has the right to dissolve the consultative council and to reform it.

Chapter Nine: General Provisions
Article 82
Without violating the contents of *Article 7* of this law, no provision of this law whatsoever can be suspended unless it is temporary, such as in a period of war or during the declaration of a state of emergency. This will be in accordance with the terms of the law.

Shura Council Statute, March 1992

Article 1
...A *shura* (consultative) council shall be established according to His law and in concordance with the Book of God and His Prophet, to retain ties of brotherhood, cooperation and faith.
Article 3
The council will consist of sixty members and a president, chosen by the king, from among people of knowledge and expertise and specialists. The duties, obligations and rights of its members and all related matters will be set by a royal order.
Article 4
Each member of the council shall be:
a) Saudi of nationality, birth and origin;
b) Known to be a person of virtue and ability;
c) Not younger than thirty years.
Article 6
Should any member of the council neglect his duties, the member shall be investigated and tried according to rules to be issued by royal order.
Article 7
If the post of a *shura* council member becomes vacant for any reason, the king chooses the person to replace him and issues a royal decree in this connection.
Article 8
Members of the council are not entitled to use their position to their advantage.
Article 9
It is not possible to retain membership in the council in conjunction with any government post or the management of

any company unless the king sees a need for this.
Article 13

The council's duration is four years starting with the date of its formation by royal decree. The new council is to be formed two months before the end of the current council. Upon the formation of a new council, it must be observed that at least half of its members must be new members who have not served in the previous council.
Article 15

The council shall give its opinion in the general policies of the states which are referred to it by the prime minister, The council's specific duties are:

a) To review the general plans for economic and social development rendering its opinion about those plans;

b) To study laws, agreements, alliances, international accords and concessions and to give its opinions concerning them;

c) To debate annual reports submitted by ministries and other government organizations and to issue its opinion concerning them.
Article 16

A quorum of two-thirds of the membership, including the president or the deputy, is required to hold a meeting. Resolutions are only valid if passed by a majority.
Article 17

Decisions of the council will be referred to the prime minister, who will transfer them to the Council of Ministers. If the views of the council are in agreement with the cabinet, the king shall approve of the decisions. If there is disagreement, the king shall make the decision.
Article 18

Laws, alliances, international agreements and concessions will be issued by royal decree after their review by the *shura* council.
Article 19

The council is empowered to form specialized committees to carry out its functions and is entitled to look into any matter that is on its agenda.
Article 20

The council can engage the expertise of any person it

wishes after the agreement of the president of the council.
Article 22

The president of the council is empowered to require from
the prime minister the presence of any government official
at the council's meetings provided the council is looking
into matters under the responsibility of that official. The
council will allow the government to invite those officials
to participate in its deliberations but they shall have no
right to vote.
Article 23

Any ten members of the council have the right to suggest
projects for new laws or to amend existing laws and to
present them to the president of the council. The president
will refer these propositions to the king.
Article 24

The president of the council has the right to ask the
prime minister to make available to the council any
documents, data or information in the possession of the
government that the council deems necessary to facilitate
its work.
Article 27

The council shall have its own budget approved by the
king. The manner of spending these budgets will be
undertaken according to royal decrees that will be issued.
Article 30

This law cannot be amended except in the manner in
which it was issued (i.e., by royal decree).[1]

King Fahd ibn Abd al-Aziz, Address, December 21, 1992

"I do not object [to] who[ever] wants to say something of
benefit to Islam, the Muslims or his country. But sometimes
there have been violations of this ancient code [the
sharia], and I do not think this is useful... Clubs and pulpits

---

[1]   The Saudi Basic Law of Government, Shura Council Statute
Decree, and the Decree on Regions Statute are available in their
entirety by the SPA, and printed in *FBIS*, March 2, 1992. The Shura
Council Statute printed here is based on the translation in *New
York Times*, March 2, 1992.

must not be exploited by one person to attack another. I believe this is absolutely unacceptable... If our doors were closed to the citizens, a person could say that he had no option but to speak his mind in the street, the mosque or anywhere else. But our doors are open and our hearts are open...

"Two years ago we began seeing things that were unfamiliar to us and were completely non-existent here. Do we accept that somebody comes to us from outside our country to direct us? No. We have our faith, and we accept directions from no one but God...Forums are no longer being used for revealing what has been established by the prophet and the book. They are now being used for worldly [i.e., political] purposes or for matters unrelated to public interest...

"I hope that efforts will be confined to giving advice for the sake of God. If, however, someone has things to say then he can always come to those in charge and speak to them in any region, in any place. As advice, this is wanted and desired. What is not desired is to bring issues out into the open. As far as bringing issues out into the open is concerned, even though in the past we have turned a blind eye to it, naturally I want it to be understood clearly that no blind eye will be turned to anything that causes damage first, to the creed, second, to the national interest and third, to anything that changes the existing situation."[1]

YEMEN

President Ali Abdallah Salih, Interview, April 29, 1993

Question: "What is your comment on the atmosphere in which the elections were held and on the available results?"

Salih: "What we are interested in is successful elections irrespective of which party wins the majority or more seats. All that the leadership was interested in has been

---

[1]   *Mideast Mirror*, December 21, 1992.

the soundness and success of this experience. As far as I know, all parties have obtained good quotas in parliament. We hope that every political organization will have a good quota in parliament. This is because we would like to have all political forces in the new parliament, especially the effective political forces, which have a weight and a political status, and which have struggled in Yemen and achieved great things for the Yemeni people, such as the realization of the Yemeni unity on May 22nd. Those have struggled until Yemen's great democratic happy day was achieved on April 27th."

Q: "The results of the elections will create a new balance at the Council of Representatives. How will this balance be reflected on the formation of the new government and on the bilateral coalition which was set up during the transitional period between the GPC [People's General Congress] and the Yemeni Socialist party (YSP), especially if the al-Islah coalition leads the YSP in the elections?
Salih: "First, as for the Council of Representatives or the new government, we perceive that, irrespective of who wins the majority, the government will be a national accord government rather than a majority government. This is because the country needs that. I believe the new government will bear major responsibilities and new tasks, especially with regard to eliminating the residue of the partition and to exercising the transitional period."

Q: "The issue of merging the two parties [GPC and YSP] was raised during the election campaign. Will this be followed up on after the announcement of the results of the elections?"
Salih: "Of course. A merger or unity between the YSP and the GPC was and continues to be raised. This will be started with the formation of a parliamentary bloc between the two parties within the framework of a future unity."[1]

---

1   Radio Monte Carlo, April 29, 1993, as printed in *FBIS*, April 30.

President Ali Abdallah Salih, Interview in al-Hayat,
May 4, 1993

"We view the success of the election process with admiration and appreciation. It was a peaceful process, thanks to all [of] our people's sense of patriotism and the interaction of all the influential political organizations and parties which cooperated to ensure the success of the elections. The rivals in the elections also lived up to the task of ensuring a sound and successful experiment. There were some violations, of course, but whatever negative aspects or violations there were, they were outweighed by the positive aspects. The negative aspects were a result of some organizational failures. There is also the question of complaints... I said on Tuesday [polling day] that any party or candidate who fails would try to contest the honesty of the elections, and that is what actually happened. I have learned that there is more than one complaint by more than one party. Every party hears that one party or another has complained, so they complain so as not to be themselves blamed for any violations. I understand that there are no more that seven main cases. The rest are all complaints by political parties about political decisions. That is harmful to the parties that complain because they blemish the successful election experiment, which, as international organizations and the press testify, was sound, successful and honest..."

Question: "Could you give us a general idea about the constitutional reforms?"
Salih: "Definition of the form of the state's presidency; ending the duplication in the work of the executive, judicial and legislative authorities; formation of a new consultative council that would have an equal elected number of representatives from the governorates as well as some efficient and influential appointees; and introduction of local government, which is one of the important tasks that will make possible the election of governors and heads of directorates. These are some of the futures of the constitutional amendments."

Q: "How do you envisage the peaceful exercise of power? Do you believe that there should be controls even for the presidency?"

Salih: "In our plan, we have limited the presidency to two terms only so that the parties and the leaders would qualify to exercise power. [Each term will last] five years.

Q: "How do you interpret the U.S. interest in the Yemeni elections and democratic experiment? Was it a pre-election interest or an encouragement surfacing after the elections became a reality?"

Salih: "There was unfair foreign media questioning of the Yemenis' ability to hold such elections and achieve unity...

"As regards the Americans, they encouraged the democratic course in our country from the beginning and welcomed the elections and their success. Their support for elections and democracy in our country was moral and informational support, not material support. Generally speaking, we are satisfied and we are very proud of the international interest, including the American interest, in our democratic experiment. We feel that the world will receive our country's successes in the democratic field with satisfaction, and that will reflect on relations between our country and many states in the world."[1]

---

[1]   *Al-Hayat*, May 4, 1993, as printed in *FBIS*, May 7.

RECENT PUBLICATIONS OF
THE WASHINGTON INSTITUTE

Enduring Partnership - Report of the Commission on U.S.-Israel Relations

PEACEWATCH Anthology - Analysis of the Arab-Israeli Peace Process from the Madrid Peace Conference to the Eve of President Clinton's Election

UN Security Council Resolution 242: The Building Block of Peace-making

Pursuing Peace: An American Strategy for the Arab-Israeli Peace Process - The final report of The Washington Institute's Strategic Study Group, with recommendations for U.S. policy in the peace negotiations by a distinguished group of Middle East experts including Samuel Lewis, Michael Mandelbaum, Peter Rodman, and Martin Indyk

Democracy and Arab Political Culture - A Washington Institute Monograph by Elie Kedourie

POLICY PAPERS SERIES

Policy Paper 35: ***Radical Middle East States and U.S. Policy*** by Barry Rubin

Policy Paper 34: ***Peace with Security: Israel's Minimal Requirements in Negotiations with Syria*** by Ze'ev Schiff

Policy Paper 33: ***Iran's Challenge to the West: How, When, and Why*** by Patrick Clawson

Policy Paper 32: ***"The Arab Street"?: Public Opinion in the Arab World*** by David Pollock

For a complete listing or to order publications, write or call:

THE WASHINGTON INSTITUTE *for Near East Policy,*
1828 L Street, NW, Suite 1050,
Washington, D.C. 20036
Phone (202) 452-0650, Fax (202) 223-5364